The Court Jester

Mansour Bahrami

in collaboration with Jean Issartel
and translated by Nigel Forrest

THE COURT JESTER

My Story

Preface and Foreword by
Yannick Noah and Ilie Nastase

The TennisMania Trust
in association with AuthorHouse

authorHOUSE®

Contents

I fled from the mullahs of Iran only to find myself stateless and homeless in Paris. Despite the setbacks, I achieved my dream: to become a professional tennis player who could compete with the best – Borg, McEnroe, Connors and the rest. I even managed to lift that legendary trophy, at the French Open....

M.B.

To my parents

To my wife Frédérique
and my sons Sam and Antoine

To my family in Iran

Paris, 2003: Yannick Noah, Tatiana Golovine, John McEnroe, Mats Wilander and me, on the occasion of a tennis concert for the Zenith Earth Children.

Iranians in Paris…. A friend called Arash, Majyar Monshipour and Ghass, an excellent painter. I was very moved when Mahyar, a six-times world boxing champion, called on me to carry his belt into the ring at the start of his final bout.

Preface by Yannick Noah

I was fifteen when I first heard his name spoken. I was studying sports science in Nice. The rising stars of French tennis at the time were called Christophe Casa and Christophe Roger-Vasselin; and they, too, were playing in Nice. They had just competed in the Galea Cup, a world championship for under-21's, and they had been knocked out by Iran. Upon their return they came to the clubhouse in Nice. I can still hear Casa saying: "It was a nonsense. They made us play blokes who were at least thirty years old. One of them had a moustache, a moustache like my grand-dad's. He was called Bahrami, that one."

A few years later I came across this famous Bahrami. His clothes had stains from the clay court, he was lunging all over the place to get the ball back, he was sweating, groaning and making animal noises. He had an incredible look, with his big belligerent moustache and socks whose elastic had seen better days. One sock was up, the other down. He seemed like a caged animal. Unintentionally, he was making everyone smile. Apart from all that, he had a special, completely incongruous way of playing tennis. He got stuck into long rallies at the back of the court and then, without anyone expecting it, he would make a backhand drop-shot. It was a wacky trick which any conventional player would never expect: and a shot which, logically, he had less than a thousand to one chance of pulling off. Except that, often, he won the point....

He was already delighting the public. It has to be said that, with him, you never got a 6 – 1, 6 – 1 score. Whether you beat him or lost, he always arranged things for it to go to three sets. If possible he would do it with one or two tie-breaks. How many times have I seen him let an opponent get the upper hand when he seemed to be beating him more easily than he fancied? Mansour is a wild lunatic. He loves this game. When he comes on court you can sense his *joie de vivre*, his sheer joy in being able to play.

When you read about his fabulous career, this extraordinary story that he has finally decided to tell, you're bound to understand more about this passion.

People often ask me what level he could have reached if he had been able to have even basic facilities, if his life had been simpler. He would probably have won many more matches and many more titles.

But, if that had happened, he would probably have become a base-line chiseller, reined in by a strict coach. If it had happened, he would have won a grand slam title and sent the crowd to sleep. If it had happened.... If it had happened, his fire would have been quashed. It would have been a tremendous waste.

Nowadays, when Bahrami's name is mentioned, you don't think of his service game or his high backhand volleys. Nor would you think of Ilie Nastase's passing spin shots. These men's talents lie elsewhere, and it's much deeper. When you say "Andy Roddick" you think of his service game, and so much the worse for him. Mansour is a piece of theatre, a magician.

Above all, he's my friend. He's a special, generous, ideal friend who shares a part of my life with irrefutable loyalty. He's the kind of friend who never forgets your birthday, or your children's, the kind of friend who treats you like royalty if you drop round, whatever the day or the time. He has always been there, in fair wind or foul. Mansour is part of my family, and it's comforting to know that. We will surely grow old together, and one day we will both be holding on to our walking-sticks, wittering on about old memories but you can be sure we'll be having fun.

Yannick Noah

In Czechoslovakia in 1976. The Iranian team which defeated the French in the Galea Cup. I was nineteen, not thirty as certain opponents believed!

Henri Leconte, Ilie Nastase and me in 2004. They had been rivals of mine, of course, but they have become like brothers to me.

Foreword by Ilie Nastase

I could say many things about Mansour. So many things, I hardly know where to begin…. Should I write about the player, this long-misunderstood genius? Should I praise his talents as a showman, his gentle madness on and off the court? Or, on the other hand, tell you what a wonderful man he is, what a generous friend whom I had the chance to meet one day when our paths crossed? But there's not much point in all that. Mansour has finally made up his mind to tell the story of his incredible life; and you will all know by the end what a cool chap he is. You'll understand what a load of courage, self-sacrifice and love it needed for him to become what he dreamed of.

Mr Bahrami has fashioned a life which matches what he decided on as a lad. Despite history and the fates which never stopped trying to dampen his passion, he has succeeded. I admire him for that. I'm sure you will feel the same when you read his story. The path he has taken is unique, and only an exceptional person could have survived the pitfalls that he has had to endure. Read his life story, and you'll never see the clown of the courts in the same way. The master for all of us, my friend.

Ilie Nastase

Prologue

I had taken my seat on the right-hand side of the chauffeur. In the back of this luxury saloon were Peter Lundgren, a former tennis player who had become Roger Federer's trainer, currently the world's number one, and Olivier Devismes, a financier who manages the financial affairs of, among others, Yannick Noah and Amélie Mauresmo. The journey from St. Anton to Geneva was going to be a long one.

Olivier, who knew a few snippets of my story from having spent many evenings with Henri Leconte, Yannick Noah, Guy Forget and me, asked me to tell him my life story, to while away the time. At first I hesitated; it would take hundreds of years to relate everything, and I didn't want to bore them with my anecdotes. In the end we found nothing better to do, so I gave in, and after five minutes they were captivated and speechless, interrupting me only to ask for more detail or to unleash commentaries such as: "Really?" "Surely not!" "That's crazy!" and so on. I had been talking for almost three hours, and they hadn't had enough, they wanted more. Even the chauffeur was enraptured and I had to tell him to concentrate on his driving. At the end of this long monologue, Peter burst out excitedly: "But, Mansour, you simply must put all that on paper: it's not a life, it's an adventure story!" I thought he was joking, but he insisted and was supported by Olivier, even by the chauffeur who acquiesced silently.

We arrived at Peter's place, late in the afternoon. He stayed behind in the car for almost half an hour, plying me with questions. That evening we went out to dinner in Geneva, Olivier, Amélie Mauresmo and me. Conversation soon turned to my life again. I took up the story once more. At the end of the meal, Amélie said to me: "Mansour, you simply have to write a book. You must write your life story. You can't let this story get lost or leave it only for your nearest and dearest." I started to think about it seriously .... I remember I began my story that night with the words: "*I was born, destitute, on 26ᵗʰ April 1956...*"

Chapter One

PARADISE LOST

I was born, destitute, on 26ᵗʰ April 1956.

It was just bad luck…. Even though it was easier for me than for the other members of my family, I have never known wealth. My relatives, on the other hand, my father in particular, slipped brutally from a life of ease to one of total poverty.

My paternal grandfather owned vast tracts of land three hundred kilometres south of Tehran, near a town called Arak. He owned an entire village by the name of Balan. It was my family who sustained the whole population. We had servants; peasants worked our lands and tended our livestock.

In Balan, about four hundred people were dependent on the Bahrami family. They grew wheat, tended sheep and cattle, and harvested the fruit in this austere and imposing landscape which was encircled by huge mountains and a jagged skyline. In that region the seasons are quite distinct: by summer, it's very hot and dry; in winter the temperature sometimes drops to twenty degrees – quite pleasant by European standards, but cool in comparison.

Until the nineteen sixties people lived in this central province of Iran as if time had stood still since the Middle Ages. No electricity, no running water, but a well in the beaten earth courtyard and oil lamps inside the house.

Even for the landowners, life was basic, and modern luxuries were not a part of everyday existence. Our single-storey house was enormous, made out of mud, a squat building with a flat roof which was used as a terrace. The house was divided into several apartments, with each one containing a branch of the family: my grandfather Karim and his wife, my father, my uncles and aunts.... In summer everyone slept on the roof to benefit from the relative coolness of the night and the birds were our alarm-clocks as the sun punctured the horizon at five-thirty in the morning. In winter a single large room, the largest in the house, was made really warm. It was in that room that everyone gathered, whether for meals or for conversation. Centre-stage in the room was the *korsi* which provided the central heating. The *korsi* was a wooden platform, about two feet high, which looked like a large chest placed flat on the ground. Inside lay the embers on a stone or metal plate. It's extremely difficult to maintain the temperature: you shouldn't put on too much coal, or the *korsi* might overheat; on the other hand, you mustn't let the fire die down too much. One has to distribute coal across the embers, then cover it with cinder-laden soil so that the burning is gradual and the heat properly diffused. Traditionally, it has been the women who tended the *korsi*'s hearth: they were the experts....

Everyone gathered round for mealtimes. The *korsi* then became a heated table. People came also for their siesta, covered by their eiderdowns; or they came to chat. In winter, family life was played out around this piece of furniture. The floor of this central room was covered with rugs on which one sat. These were the only manifestations at that time of a family's wealth. There were no other pieces of furniture – no tables, no armchairs, just rugs. But what rugs! They would be made of silk (which had taken months to produce) or of incredibly soft wool. Around the *korsi*, you propped yourself up on silk cushions; you were enveloped by your eiderdown; and you let yourself be taken over by the heat. By the smell, too.

The *korsi* gave off a smell difficult to re-create or to describe. It was a smell of smoke, commingled with the aromas of spicy food and of rugs.... it generated a sweet perfume which, for me, is unforgettable.

Meals were conducted according to unchanging traditions. Each person sat in his or her appointed place, determined once and for all according to one's age and status in the family. Before I was born, my grandfather Karim had pride of place, my father on his right and then other adult males. After that came the women and children.

Iranian cuisine could never be described as highly varied. Put simply, the poor would eat a single dish, mutton stew, while the well-to-do would place on the *korsi* skewers of mutton and veal, rice, various sauces, yoghourt with cucumber, different kinds of salad and, in summer, fruit. Iranian food is very spicy, scented, but not piquant. Each person chooses for himself and serves himself. You create your own mixture ....desserts don't exist; little cucumbers, very refreshing ones, were often used to finish a meal, whilst pears, oranges or apples can be eaten at any stage.

In Iran you drink tea at any time too, wherever you happen to be. In the Bahrami household there was a samovar, placed on the *korsi*, on the go twenty-four hours a day. There was a basket of fruit within easy reach as well; business issues, the future and family problems were discussed, cup in hand, as we crunched on baby cucumbers. It was by the *korsi*, as everyone was drinking tea, that my grandfather announced to his sons that they would have to give up their lands.

Chapter Two

CONSPIRACY AND EXILE

Some years after the Second World War, a terrible drought gripped the Arak region for several years in a row. At the end of this period of skinny cows (if you'll forgive the expression), one of my grandfather's best friends asked him to lend him money and act as guarantor of a bank loan to get his business underway. However, this "friend of thirty years' standing" finally disavowed his debts and, with the complicity of the local police, refused to repay the loan. The bank seized everything from my grandfather. Land, houses, cattle and the harvest were taken. Everything.... it was an outrageous rip-off and a dreadful conspiracy. It led straight to my grandfather's death, scarcely a year after I was born. He died of heartbreak.

My father, Rahim, had to leave his lands and scuttle off to Tehran to feed his family. He was sixty when I was born; and he had to start again from scratch. At his pensioner's age, he became a gardener in Tehran's biggest sports complex. This was for a salary of the equivalent of thirty pounds a month.

Of course, I learnt all this only over a period of time, in the course of conversations between my parents, between my father and his brother ....

When my mother told me once (my father didn't want to discuss it) that the Bahramis used to be "rich and respected people" I didn't believe it. Just imagine: she spoke to me of servants, a cook and governesses, of retainers who would prepare my father's bath and serve dinner and of lands as far as the eye could see, belonging to the Bahrami dynasty. No, I couldn't believe it: "How could you make up these stories? Haven't you seen where we're living? And you're speaking to me about servants? You're lying to me!" I knew, on the other hand, that a mother doesn't lie to her youngest son. Not my mother, anyway.

Regular visitors proved to me that she was telling the truth. In the cellar with its beaten earth floor, beneath the north stand of the football stadium, we occasionally had visits from people who had arrived from the south, from Balan. They would kiss the hand of my father and would treat him with a deference that was incredible. What I couldn't understand was: why did they kiss the hand of a gardener? Why did they lower their gaze when talking to him and treat me as if I was the crown prince? To what was I the heir? My father's rake and bucket? We were living as a squashed-up six-some in a hundred square foot hovel, and these people from the south entered our place as if it were holy ground. They were the family's former farm workers, former servants who had seen my brothers as they grew up, who had wept upon the death of my father's first wife, celebrated at his second wedding, then wept again at the funeral of my grandfather, having greeted my birth as a stellar blessing....

My father was only a piece of low-life in Tehran, a poor gardener. But in their eyes he was the master, the boss. In my eyes he was a tired old man who had to slave away twelve hours a day to feed us. I was worried I would see him collapse from old age and over-work. I must have been only nine or ten months old when he had no choice but to flee to Tehran with my mother and my two brothers. Three years later my little sister was born. To this already quite sizeable family you have to add the two children from my mother's first marriage (her first husband had died) and the son my father had had before meeting my mother. Fortunately, my half-brothers and my half-sister had already grown up and didn't live with us in our overcrowded room. They had got married and made their own lives in Tehran. Despite all that we lived as a kind of community. Alongside our room – I should say alongside our hole – there were five other similar dwellings. You went down four steps under the stand in the stadium and arrived at our twelve-by-nine-foot hovels.

In the summer, when it was really hot, the six large families would take their mattresses outside, sprinkle water on the ground to make the air cooler and all sleep there. It might seem pretty terrible to you, this lack of privacy, but for lads like me it was a fine way of life. We adored sleeping in the open air, or rather pretending to sleep while listening out for the conversations of the adults. We were happy.... I was happy.

The first photo of me. I was ten and am here with my ball boy friends, Ali, Hadi and Ali Reza, at the Amjadieh tennis club. We behaved as if we were playing in the final of a great tournament.

Chapter Three

AMJADIEH

My earliest memories of the sports complex called Amjadieh where I spent the whole of my childhood evoke, even today, a marvellous aroma, like the smell of an oasis. For a young lad it was paradise. I lived in a park entirely given over to sports and leisure. Iran's finest football stadium was there, and all the major national and international matches took place there. There was also a second pitch for training sessions, four or five basketball courts and two gymnasia. Then there was an Olympic swimming pool, a pool for public use and yet another for kids. The public swimming pool closed at five o'clock, and we, the kids of Amjadieh, then took it over. We could be seen warming up, a quarter of an hour before closing time, ready to jump into the water once the green light was shown. We loved swimming but, above all, we had some tasks to do: we would swim the circuit of the pool, looking for jewellery and coins which people had accidentally dropped into the water. Not a summer's day passed without one of us bringing back a watch, a ring or a necklace. The pool, for us, was like a great treasure hunt. However, for us, there was something even better, and more lucrative: the great Iranian football championship matches. The stands were made of slatted wood; and we slipped underneath, hoping for plenty of goals. Each time the score changed, spectators would shout out, jump up, raise their arms and, inevitably, let slip lighters, wallets, watches or gold chains! And there, under the stand, we conducted our business.

Amjadieh…. In this sports complex, three times the size of

9

Roland-Garros, there were streams of water so pure you just had to kneel down beside them to drink. Tehran is built on the plain at the foot of the mountains, and the water in those streams came straight down from the mountain peaks. I remember the sound of those little rivers, and the taste of the water when, after hours of kicking a ball or running after the other kids, I leant down to scoop up, two-handed, this crystal-clear liquid. Now in my fifties, I still have that delicious freshness in my mouth. I just have to shut my eyes and I can hear the ripples, breathe in their delicate perfume. I remember also the brambles which grew at the edges of the shooting range. We feasted on their sugar-laden fruit. It was fabulous. My childhood, despite the poverty and the vexations, was also filled with good experiences.

I played ping-pong, swam every day, did some boxing and played volleyball. The one thing I wasn't allowed to play was tennis ….The thirteen courts, with the central one encased by stands capable of holding about four hundred spectators, were open only to privileged people, the Iranian middle-class. We, the children of Amjadieh's staff, were allowed to do anything, go anywhere, except on those courts. You don't have to look further than that for the source of my passion for tennis. It sprang from a prohibition.

I didn't realise how sad, or rather how melancholy, my father had become. With the benefit of hindsight and of advancing age, the details now take on a meaning, and I can remember his face and some of his attitudes. How could he have smiled, seeing the conditions under which his family were living? The lavatories – a simple hole in the ground serving four families – the lack of showers, so for bathing we had to resort to the public *hammam*…. and the meals – often my mother would send me out to look for herbs for the soup, a kind of dandelion which I would pick from the lawn bordering the stream. Twice a week I went with her to buy a little meat at one of the stalls just outside the sports ground. She cooked well, but with little. She prepared *abgousht*, our basic dish, the staple of the poor. Literally *abgousht* means "water and meat". It's like a mutton hotpot, with onions and chick-peas. When guests came round she would add a little water so that everyone could share. Twice a month she cooked rice with meat and an aubergine sauce. That was good; but there was something even better. For me it was watermelon.

There was a round pond near our little hovel. When my father brought a watermelon back, he would dangle it in the pond to cool it for when we came to eat. When I heard the splash of that fruit I knew that I was going to have the best, the sweetest, of foods. For me that was a feast day. Then, every two or three months, my mother would buy a water-ice which I had to share with my little sister. On those days my father actually smiled, seeing us happy.

He was a serious believer, a Shi'ite Muslim like ninety per cent of the Iranian population, and he pushed me to follow the precepts of the prophet Mohammed without in any way forcing me into it. He went to mosque twice a week and prayed five times a day, with my mother; but he rapidly gave up the idea of demanding I do likewise. These devotions made an impression on me, but I couldn't see myself getting up before sunrise to kneel, facing east and beginning the day in prayer. Occasionally I trembled a bit at the prospect of ending up in hell rather than in the promised green paradise where the finest fruit trees grew and the sweetest women were to be found. Nevertheless, I didn't change my ungodly ways. I did respect his faith and the sacrifices he made; but I didn't feel the need to behave like him. In this respect, as it has turned out, I haven't changed.

Unfortunately for me, whether I was a practising Muslim or not had nothing to do with it: I did have to be circumcised. This event was presented to me as a great feast and an unforgettable moment. I instinctively felt that there had to be more to it; and I discussed it with friends of mine who had already gone through it. Then I understood. I understood that the barber who cut our hair would use his scissors to cut something else! He had a second role in our society, a role more noble but also more painful for his "clients", using the same pair of scissors for cutting hair as for circumcisions. In those days there were no antiseptics and no anaesthetic on offer. When the "great day" arrived, I ran away.

I had hidden myself behind a wooden storeroom where the Amjadieh gardeners kept seeds and tools. I was waiting to see what would happen, when I heard someone come up behind me and call my name. It had taken two hours, apparently, to track me down. Two hours during which I had done nothing but run. When they finally laid their hands on me, I just fainted. I had collapsed from exhaustion. My father and brother scooped me up; the barber said "Look at that bird up there." And that was it. My circumcision had passed off painlessly because I was already semi-conscious!

It was not long after this episode, before my sixth birthday, when I started as a ball boy for the big-wigs who played tennis there. I got up around five o'clock and would go and wait for my clients at the entrance to the clubhouse. Obviously I wasn't the only one. All the kids at Amjadieh – there were around fifty of us aged between three and ten – did the same job. On average we earned about ten cents an hour; and these tips were always useful to top up the family kitty. I would be picking up balls until eight o'clock in the morning, when I sloped off to school. When I got back, around four o'clock, I gulped down my favourite tea (a tomato and a delicious kind of bread called *barbari*), and then, little rebel that I was, I earned my crust closely observing this game that made me dream.

After nightfall I got back to the "house" under the football stadium stand with the equivalent of forty pence in my pocket, which I handed over to my mother. She would hand me back a tiny share of that, two or three pence, telling me "I'm only giving you that; but if you don't bring anything back tomorrow you'll still have some coins.... " I didn't complain. It was normal. The only thing which annoyed me was the mean types, those who had given me only a few pence, whereas my regulars usually gave me three times as much.

The skinflints – we did everything we could to avoid them. We watched out for our clients to arrive, and as soon as one was recognised, the cluster of boys fragmented instantly. But, oh dear!, the man in charge of the court bookings always managed to get hold of one of us to work for peanuts. We had to keep quiet if we were to be allowed to come back the next day. The worst of all was that the most demanding clients were also the meanest and the ones who would insult, threaten or even raise a hand to us. At that time, in Iran, certain people enjoyed a kind of untouchability. Those without moral boundaries took advantage of this to please themselves and behave like barbarians. Happily, the good clients were in the majority. The ones I liked best weren't necessarily the ones who would give me the most money. I liked the good players. I just loved watching them. It was thanks to them that I could study different techniques – forehand, backhand, volley and service. I never went straight home after these hours of working. I held a piece of wood or a broom and hit balls against a wall. I copied the strokes I'd observed on the court and hit the balls with all my might. I adored it.

My favourite season was winter. They emptied the Olympic swimming pool; and for me it became the most wonderful of tennis courts. I climbed down the ladder and played facing the highest wall, where the depth was three metres. That's how my career began: with a broom on the floor of a swimming pool. At night I dreamt of rackets. I pictured myself playing with a Slazenger, striking long forehand shots, chipping backhands and driving smashes with all my might....

A racket: what would I not have given for a racket?

One summer's day, when I must have been ten years old, I was waiting for clients, not feeling too hopeful. These really hot afternoons in Iran were rarely devoted to sport. Everyone was taking a siesta; the shopkeepers would draw their curtains, and no-one reappeared before four o'clock. I, on the other hand, preferred hitting a ball against a wall with a broom, rather than lazing in the shade. I was secretly hoping that there wouldn't be a client coming to ask me to act as his ball boy. The one who arrived was a very beautiful woman, aged about forty: the wife of a big-wig. She knew me in the way that she knew all the kids at Amjadieh hanging around the entrance for the privilege of picking up the balls. She asked me:

"Mansour, what are you doing? Why are you playing with a broomstick?"

"Well, it's better than playing with my hand. Sometimes I use a shovel; but a broom's better; I can hit the ball better.…"

She answered me with a tone both astounded and naïve:

"But, Mansour, why don't you play with a racket? Tennis is played with a racket, you know, not a broom."

"I haven't got any money to buy a racket. Rackets are expensive.…"

In those days a racket would have cost about two months' wages for my father. She simply said:

"It's impossible, Mansour. You must have a racket. Tomorrow I'll bring you a racket!"

There were tears in my eyes. I wanted to kiss her. She had become for me more revered than a saint. That night I didn't sleep, trying to imagine which racket she would bring for me. I dreamt of a Slazenger; but I didn't want to fixate too much on that, telling myself that a Dunlop or a Gauthier would be fabulous enough. The next day I was up at four o'clock in the morning and I waited for her. When I saw her parking her car, I rushed towards her. She smiled at me, saying that she was very sorry: she had forgotten. "But tomorrow," she promised me, "tomorrow I will bring it without fail." That night my dream was a bit more troubled. She strung me along for three months; every morning I was waiting for her. When she arrived, I rushed towards her. Each time she had forgotten. But, as she made the promises, I was always there the following morning. My dream was within her power: I couldn't believe that she wouldn't honour it. After all, I hadn't asked anything of her.…

One morning her smile was more open than usual. I saw her looking at me from a long way off and coming towards me. My heart jumped: this time, surely, she had brought it with her. I leapt at her:

"So, you've brought my racket?" She said she hadn't.

Before I started to cry she added, "But I've got something else for you!"

14

Out of her bag she pulled a doll! A poxy little doll! I was furious. I insulted her and threw the doll on the ground. I called her a tart and told her to go and screw herself.

She was horrified and told me again and again, "Mansour, what's got into you? How can you say such things?"

"I didn't ask for anything," I replied, "You've been promising me a racket for months, and you give me a doll. I'm not a girl, I'm a tennis player!"

And this tennis player had to return to the bottom of the emptied swimming pool to hit balls with the end of a piece of wood, dreaming that one day he would walk on to the centre court at Roland-Garros – the most famous clay courts in the world.

Chapter Four

MY FATHER ABDOLRAHIM

I must have been barely twelve years old when the sports minister was sacked. That event wouldn't have been of any interest to me if it hadn't had dramatic consequences for our existence. The new minister, one of the Shah's generals, decided to drive out all the families living at Amjadieh. Why? No-one ever told us. My father was allowed to carry on working as a gardener, but he had to leave the hovel where we had lived those past twelve years. Overnight, all the families living there found themselves without a roof over their heads. We packed our bags and moved the few bits of furniture we had. We found refuge in the garden of my half-sister, my mother's oldest daughter. To call it a garden was a bit of an exaggeration: it was more a piece of beaten earth next to the house where she lived with her husband and children. Luckily it was summer, and it wasn't too painful to live outside, under the stars. I was used to that and loved it. My recollection of this period, however, is not one of a carefree existence. My parents were wondering what they could do to avoid being on the street by the autumn. My father was out from morning till night trying to find a solution, some land, some money ….We had been at my half-sister's for more than two months. Then, one day, my father came back with a smile on his lips. With all his scrimping and saving, and with the help of a loan, he had bought a small house. Our first house! Small, a long way from his place of work, but it was ours. He was proud; that much was visible in his eyes. So I was proud, too. Proud of him, proud of my father, this little gardener who had succeeded in providing a roof for his family, despite his advanced age, his fatigue, despite the blows of fate which seemed to rain down on him.

In our garden, when I was seventeen. I'm with my mother Bibi and my father.

But it was so far away from the stadium....At least ten kilometres. Nevertheless, I went there every day with him, before and after school, and for the whole day during the school holidays. I played tennis against a wall with my stick, and I tried to earn some money while he was working so hard. He began at eight in the morning and finished after six in the evening. For lunch we often shared an aubergine which he would grill over a wood fire. These were good times for me; I felt close to him. I felt a bit sad too, seeing how he was worn out. And so it was that, after lunch, I would help him sweep up dead leaves or to tend the trees. However, whatever I did, by the end of the day he was exhausted before even starting the journey home. To save money, he refused to take the bus home; he was often suffering from hypoglycaemia, not able to think clearly, walking with difficulty, a grimace of pain etched on his lined, pallid face which had borne its cross for so long that it seemed normal to him .... I would beg him to take the bus, but every time he would reply, "We'll walk, we'll walk."

He was almost seventy and staggered after a few kilometres. And we walked on without exchanging a word. He was unable to speak, lost in his thoughts. I'm sure it was impossible for him to stay anchored in reality. He wouldn't have survived if he had faced things head-on, if he had seen his state of dishevelment. I'm not even sure that he was thinking of anything in particular. It was enough for him simply to put one foot in front of the other to conserve energy, to keep whatever he had left to allow him to get back and collapse on to his bed. Every evening I was convinced he wouldn't make it. Every evening I was thinking he would die, there and then, in front of my very eyes. So I walked behind him, staying close. I had tears in my eyes. Sometimes he was on the point of falling over. On those occasions I would catch his arm, and his spirits would lift as he said "But why are you holding on to me like that?"

I replied without being able to look into his empty stare. "I'm sorry, Papa, I almost fell and I caught on to your arm...." I was too afraid to upset him, to wound his pride when he was already suffering physically. I was scared that something would happen to him, and that he would tumble once and for all. When we got home we were both dead-beat. And so he paid for this house by ruining his health even more day by day.

My mother did what she could, but she was old too, and her days were dedicated mainly to the search for an evening meal. There was always an evening meal, often frugal and rarely including meat but, still, we were fed.

I was still giving my mother my ball boy's tips, but then I decided to launch some small commercial operations on those evenings when there were football matches. I bought bread which I cut into small pieces and sold at the entrance to the stadium, at a hefty mark-up. I sold fresh water too, which I had collected from the streams. I didn't have fixed prices, so the skinflints paid me nothing, whereas the majority of the fans gave me a coin. With my mates I had a kitty which allowed us to graduate to a bigger enterprise. We bought bottles of soda wholesale and sold them at a profit. I did everything I could to bring some extra money home, as well as to keep a little for myself. I managed to buy a broken-down bike which my father and I repaired. That changed my life as I was able to travel to and from the stadium far more quickly....

My sisters Esmat and Efat; and my niece Nasreen

Chapter Five

ATTEMPTED MURDER

It was an old Jack Kramer racket, made of wood and without its strings. Norooz, a good player whom I knew, wanted to get rid of it, and he sold it to me for something like fifteen pence. I was twelve, and I had grasped the chance of my life, or at least the first one. I scavenged some string from a dustbin and some old catgut from the clubhouse, and I strung it after a fashion. I made a knot outside the bottom hole, pulled with all my might and drove in a nail across the hole at the top. After all that, my first racket must have weighed two kilos! It was to become so famous that a replica of it is now on display at Roland-Garros ....

My first racket! I sauntered around everywhere with it, and with so much pride that it made everyone laugh. Especially Shirzad Akbari. He was ten years older than me, one of the best Iranian players and a member of the Davis Cup squad. Shirzad was my idol. When he was playing in a match, I would shout encouragements like a madman. I just couldn't stand seeing him lose. I adored his game; he was always on the attack, a real terrier. I watched closely to try and copy his strokes and his style. That was the way I learned, no coach, no one-to-one lessons, I observed and copied, hour after hour at the bottom of my swimming pool.

With two friends from the Amjadieh Club. Asghar Khodai (on
the left) is now a tennis coach at the Longchamp Tennis Club,
near Paris: Shirzad Akbari (on the right) is the one who gave me
my first racket.

When Shirzad arrived at the club, on his bike, I rushed forward to park it for him. A magical moment! For one thing I could use the bike a bit, and then glowed with pride performing a service for the champion. All the Davis Cup matches played on home ground were at the Amjadieh courts.

I, professional ball boy, was summoned for the occasion. When it was his turn to play, I was entranced. I must have been a pretty mediocre ball boy but a really excellent supporter. Once, Romania came to play Iran, and I was given an earful by Ilie Nastase. He found me a bit too partial and exuberant.... Now, years later, Ilie has become one of my best friends.

But to come back to Shirzad. He trained at Amjadieh and also gave private lessons to earn a living; I was his official ball boy when he was giving lessons. I picked up balls from every corner of the court and passed them back to him by hand. I did my utmost to bring about various tricks to produce bizarre, surprising deflections of the ball. He hated it and said that it would be the last time he would choose me: nevertheless, each time, he did pick me again. One morning, when I had already had my nailed-up racket for several weeks, he said: "Mansour, if you pass back the balls to me today in the proper way, flat along the ground, without any pranks, I'll offer you something at the end of the lesson." I'm not sure what got into me, but I obeyed his instruction, and at the end of the lesson he gave me one of his rackets. It was a Slazenger.... It was weird, I had waited seven years for a racket, and then, in the course of a few weeks I had got two. For me, that was like becoming a professional!

The snag was that a pro' with two rackets can't be content simply to play alone in the bottom of a swimming pool. One summer's day, in the middle of August, I crossed the line and joined a friend of mine who had access to the courts.

There was no-one in the clubhouse and no-one nearby. It was forty-five degrees, and everything was quiet, as if the birds and the wind were taking their siesta too. My partner was two or three years older than me, but I was expecting to beat him. I stepped on to the court in trepidation but, at the same time, I felt big and strong. I had already lived this moment in hundreds of nights of dreams. I had my two rackets tucked under my arm and, in my mind, I had wormed my way through to the centre court at Roland-Garros to play the final of the French Open. This was 1968, I was twelve years old, a metre and a half high, but felt like a professional. Just imagine: - two rackets!

We had been knocking up for less than three minutes when four security guards came out of nowhere and surrounded me. I hadn't seen them approaching. The senior one was called Alireza Rezaï, and he was the stadium's watchman at the time. He was a sad case. He was still alive but might not be by the time you read these lines of mine. I think I have forgiven him for what he did to me. However, that took a long time ….

He deliberately set out to kill me. I have never understood why. He could simply have said to me: "Get out!" and I would have complied. He was accompanied by three guards, but it was his presence alone which scared me. He looked at me with an evil eye. He was built like a mountain. Without uttering a word he caught me, lifted me up with one arm, took me out of the court and hurled me with all his might to the ground, near the stream which ran between the tennis courts. I was stunned. But then I saw him bend down, felt him catch me again, hold me up, above his head and throw me for a second time down on the ground. He did it again, five or six times, and I was barely conscious. I was bleeding, my head spinning, my vision was fuzzy and I couldn't hear anything ….But I was clearly thinking: "He's going to kill me. Today, Mansour, you are going to die. Perhaps you're already dead?" But no, he left me there, in a pool of blood which was running slowly into the stream. I couldn't move, had one eye closed, but the other could see, through a blood-filled mist, this monster of a man heading for my two rackets. I understood what that meant and registered fear. I begged him and I think I was crying out, but could hardly hear, as if my own voice were coming from too far away. But he had heard me, for sure, because he turned towards me once he had picked up my two rackets. He looked at me, smiling.

I shouted "No-o-o-o!!" but, still looking me up and down, he placed the rackets over a step and jumped on them. They were completely smashed. My life, too, and I fainted. I would have preferred him to have killed me.

I found out from others the sequel to all this. My brother's best friend, Ezat Nematy, a former Davis Cup player who lived just behind the courts, had heard me crying. He came out to fetch me and carried me to his home where I was given first aid. Shirzad, my older brother who had come to have lunch at our home, apparently saw red. He was quite sturdy but far from being as strong as Alireza Rezaï. Nevertheless, he went round to Alireza's place and gave him a terrific thrashing. He broke three of his teeth which Alireza has never had replaced. Shirzad wanted to kill him, but five people intervened. He was shouting: "I swear I will kill you if you lay a hand ever again on my brother. You stopped me playing tennis, and you want to do the same to my brother Mansour. But this time, I won't let you do it. Mansour's going to play: I'm telling you straight, he's going to play! I'm telling you you'll let him go on the courts, and you're going to leave him in peace...."

It was just my brother urging me not to give up. All the others preached to me: "Mansour, stop your dreaming! Tennis isn't for you. You need to choose a real job. Why don't you become a cobbler like your brother? Tennis isn't right for you; let it drop."

But the more they advised me to give up tennis, the more I dreamt of it and spent my time knocking up against a wall, using my broomstick once more.

The first tournament in which I played.
I am in the middle. I'm so proud of having won the trophy!
Morteza (bottom left) was my best friend: he lived next to our
home. Each of the kids had a nickname. Hussein (holding the
cup, on the right) was called Gagarin.

Chapter Six

BETRAYAL

Against all expectations, my beating-up had caused quite a stir at the club and even beyond. Those in charge, who were high-ups in the community, took up my cause. They all found what had happened to be disgraceful, but no-one took the decision to open up the courts to the inmates of Amjadieh, nor, for that matter, to discipline Alireza Rezaï. It was just a sterile collection of virtuous sentiments. Even so, the idea of letting us play began to make some progress. You shouldn't get the idea that the near-killing of a common urchin could change society's moral values. If there was to be a change, it would be for much more mundane reasons. The executives of the Iranian Tennis Federation were becoming aware that their best players were ageing, and of the lack of young blood to replace them. Results were needed. The Shah, like all heads of state, believed that victories in sport channelled the vague desires of a competitive populace into nationalistic fervour. He liked sport and the sight of the Iranian flag hoisted aloft at international competitions. In Iran, as elsewhere, a federation without top-flight players is liable to disappear. Most of the Federation's leaders were concerned neither with the players nor the game itself, but their position gave them a social status, some benefits in kind and the feeling that they could "pull strings", even though these strings were as pathetic and inconsequential as the game of tennis in Iran at that time. Therefore the decision was taken to organise a revival.

There weren't too many ways of finding young players capable of becoming tennis professionals. The ball-tapping offspring of middle-class families considered tennis to be a recreation and wouldn't have considered it a profession. They needed to become lawyers, doctors, generals or businessmen. The bosses of the Federation and the Sports Ministry thought this through to its natural conclusion.

As all the best tennis players in Iran were, like me, former ball boys, gardeners' or wardens' sons who had learnt to play by themselves, it was decided that the gates to the courts should be opened wide to the most talented kids at Amjadieh. I was the first to be chosen. I didn't dare believe that my dream had started to come true and that "my career" had been launched. To some extent I was right to think that way....

At the beginning, however, everything went perfectly. The bosses at the club summoned me and gave me two new rackets, saying: "Mansour, you can play when you want, and on the court of your choice. These rackets, we're giving them to you, not lending them – they're yours." Two other kids who had lived in the cellars next to mine were treated to the same favours. I was now thirteen, and it was only at that pivotal age that I could begin to train anything like seriously. I was no longer a ball boy but a tennis player. Just thinking that made me very proud... and much better off! After twelve months, the beginning of my fourteenth year, I had become Iranian champion in my age group, and for the group above that. At the club, adults were paying me to hit with them. I wasn't a teacher, yet I was getting the equivalent of fifty pence an hour. I was much in demand.

That didn't prevent me from training hard: there wasn't much time for other things, and my school-work suffered as a result. I can't say that getting bad marks upset me. I didn't have anything to prove at school. I was fulfilled by playing in every daylight hour that I could. Everything was going O.K. I was happy.

Aged sixteen. I'm playing on the court where I was beaten up.

One afternoon, having worked up a sweat while training, I was sauntering alongside the courts waiting for the chance to start playing. But there had been no sign of anyone for several hours, and I knew I would not be able to add to my nest-egg before the next morning when Hadi, a friend of mine who is today a tennis pro' in Holland, came and suggested a dice game with me. In Iran dice games such as backgammon are very popular; people often play for money but, at that age, we simply played for the fun of it.

So there we were, sitting next to the stream, under a weeping willow, rolling dice. The man who handled the court bookings passed by. He stood for a couple of minutes staring at us, then left. Two hours later, as I was on my way home, I was told to report to the clubhouse.

There the secretary-general of the Iranian Tennis Federation asked me: "Mansour, is it true you were playing dice this afternoon?" Of course I said that I had.

"You admit your mistake, and that's good, but it doesn't alter the fact that you are suspended *sine die* and you are no longer allowed to enter the club. So, off you go, and don't let me see you again!"

I was devastated and didn't believe it but, seeing that he was being serious I protested: "But what have I done wrong? Why are you saying such a thing to me?"

"Mustn't play dice," he said. "Gambling is forbidden here: it's a serious vice which we cannot tolerate. Your attitude isn't compatible with what is required of a tennis player. Too bad for you: you've been given your opportunity, and you've thrown it away. No more tennis for you."

Today, all these years later, I still don't understand why he did that, when everyone in Iran played with dice or at cards and gambled on all of that, and not for peanuts, either .... I suppose I'll never know.

Even worse than my threatened suspension was that I hadn't yet received the trophies for my two titles as Iranian national champion in the fourteen- and sixteen-year old categories. There was to have been an official ceremony at the club two months after the championships, and now I was forbidden from going. How could I collect my cups? This question was gnawing at me. I couldn't believe that they had thrown me out of my dream world in such an uncompromising way. I was sure that, at some time or another, I would be able to return; but I was wondering whether that day would come before or after the award ceremony.

Days and weeks passed without anyone putting an end to my banishment. I clung on stubbornly, kicking my heels every day from dawn to dusk at the entrance to the club and, every time one of the bosses passed by, would beg him to let me in. The answer was always the same: "No, Mansour, you won't ever come back. Get yourself a job. Tennis is not for you." I just couldn't accept that and felt I had been unfairly treated. Did they want new young players or didn't they?

After several weeks, I reluctantly agreed, on the advice of my brother Shirzad, to start an apprenticeship as a cabinet-maker. The days were long, and I earned fifty pence a day, exactly what I had been earning each hour playing tennis. I lasted a few days and then told myself: "Shit! This isn't what I want to do; this way of life holds no interest for me at all. For me, life is about tennis." And I went back to begging outside the club.

On the day of the awards ceremony, I was sure they would lift my ban. I didn't dare hope it would be a complete reversal, simply that they would at least let me take part in the ceremony long enough to collect my trophies in front of the crowd. Some hope! The first trophies of my life were given to me, hurriedly, on the street, by the Federation secretary as he was leaving and after everyone else had gone.

I had seen the other kids, the ones I had beaten, leave with joy in their eyes, having picked up chocolate medallions for being finalists. They looked happy, having received their honours. As the winner, I had earned a quick "Here, take this, after all, it's you who won this cup", without even a handshake or a smile.

My exile lasted three months in total. Three months that were longer than eternity. Even today, it feels to me as if I was banned for several years. Finally, the bosses of the Federation were abruptly replaced, for reasons I didn't understand. A certain Majid Alam, a close friend of the Shah, was appointed president. He brought in a vice-president called Arsham Yessaï. He was my first patron. I behaved towards him as I had done towards his predecessors: I begged him to let me back in. He looked at me in a funny sort of way, smiled and said: "But Mansour, of course you can come back. Why wouldn't you be able to? I'd like to know who would dare stop you!"

He knew it was the best way to draw a line under the past, and it was a way of saying to me: "This injustice never happened. Play tennis and forget that anyone ever tried to prevent you. That'll never happen again. Play...."

Chapter Seven

WIMBLEDON

If there was one man who was responsible for putting tennis on the map in Iran, it's Mr Yessaï. He handled everything, from the élite to the kids to the population at large. He put all his intelligence, his energy and his personality into serving the game and its development.

Thus, two years after his appointment as vice-president of the Federation, Mr Yessaï succeeded in convincing Majid Alam, Federation president and close ally of the Shah, that those on whom Iran's best hopes were pinned should be helped financially to travel and to experience international competition in order to improve their game. At the time – I was sixteen – I was playing in only three or four tournaments a year, and all of those were in Iran. In fact, I was coming up against, and beating, the same opponents, and the only thing which spurred me on to improve my game were the infrequent defeats I suffered when I came up against the players from the Iranian Davis Cup squad, who were in their thirties.

The system which was devised to help us consisted of private patronage. Rich Iranians interested in the game were asked to become sponsors of the best juniors. Three men decided to help me. Soon, one of them, Mr Bozorgebrahimi, dropped out. The other two, who were bigger contributors, remained. Even today, I keep in touch with the first of these, Jahangir Nazemian. At the time, he owned the equivalent of a gold-mine, because he was the only one who provided heavy machinery for civil engineering – cranes, bulldozers and so on. He was involved in all the country's big construction projects. His firm was the JCB of Iran.

Changing ends in a Galea Cup match. I am listening to the words of my captain, Arsham Yessaï

The second of my patrons has unfortunately died. He was an electrical engineer and the importer of electronic equipment. Mr Dowlatshahi, who, like Jahangir Nazemian, was a tennis player, saw the game mainly as an aesthetic experience. Both liked my style, and that's what made them agree to cover all my expenses. But I had to provide tennis coaching and agree to play handicap matches against all those who dared take me on. I wagered all I could to beat rich citizens by playing the match with a limp or with an unstrung racket: I struck the ball only with the wood of the racket, even serving, and pocketed the proceeds of my bets. I was virtually unbeatable at this little game, and so I had to devise other handicaps: one eye blindfolded, an arm tied behind my back, both legs tied together, which meant I had to jump rather than run.... but these shows soon annoyed Mr Nazemian and Mr Dowlatshahi. In their eyes, this was clowning, not tennis, and they were adamant they didn't want me to vegetate by doing coaching and showing off with an unstrung racket. They were paying my wages in order for me to play, practise and improve .... I didn't have the right to take on bets except with them. We played doubles, me partnering Mr Dowlatshahi, and a pal of mine, Kambiz Drafshijavan, whose standard was equal to mine, pairing up with Mr Nazemian. They wagered enormous sums, but the bet was only between the two of them. I couldn't match that, so I would stake fifty dollars.

In Switzerland with my team-mates and George Aftandelian (second left) who was to be chosen as my guardian at Wimbledon in 1973.

Mr Ali Dowlatshahi with his sons Mehbod and Farbod and his grandson Aria.

They gave me bonuses, to win or to lose, as the case might be, but that didn't stop me doing my utmost to win with whomever I was partnering. I think they appreciated this loyalty that they found in Kambiz and me. We were the top pairing in the country and indeed in the whole of Asia. As a twosome we had not lost a single match in Iran or in Asia. We weren't even beaten often by European players who came to Iran. At the age of sixteen Kambiz and I were the unshakeable Davis Cup doubles partnership. He had started playing earlier than I had – his father was one of the tennis coaches at Amjadieh – but, because he was gifted at all kinds of sport, his talent was a bit diluted. He had even competed, at the age of fifteen, in a few Iranian first division football matches before opting clearly for tennis. What really gripped him, however, was betting. He was challenging everyone, all the time, to a bet. If he met a volley-ball player and provoked him enough, he would suggest betting on a game, with a stake of fifty dollars. He would ask for five points' advantage to start with, and usually, even in sports he had played only once or twice in his life, he would win the wager. He simply had them in his blood, sports and betting. Even today, in his fifties, he spends his time betting on almost anything....

In Manila in 1974 during a tournament where I was crowned Junior Asian Champion.

Thanks to my sponsors, to their financial support and to the serious attitude they demanded of me, I improved day by day. My technique evolved, and, with the extra work, my strength and endurance improved too. When I was seventeen my sponsors called me in, having seen my progress, and said: "Mansour, it's time to end our doubles matches and wagering. You should be setting out on a real career, and we've decided you should go and play in tournaments abroad for eight to ten months a year. We will give you what you need for that, and in exchange we simply ask that you promise us to do your best to continue to improve and become the best player you possibly can."

I promised them I would. I remember the first big foreign tournament, some months after my benefactors had decided to sponsor me....

In their wisdom, the Federation sent me to play in the junior tournament at Wimbledon! I knew nothing about Wimbledon except that I had heard they played on grass. I was very excited to play for the first time on this surface. Excited but also apprehensive and anxious. The Federation had delegated a good former player, George Aftandelian to look after me, and I did indeed need looking after. I didn't speak a single word of English and would have been incapable of surviving in London without a companion.

The organisers of this most famous tournament in the world had booked for me, as for all the juniors, a room in a shabby hostel called King George's House. Once we had checked in and unpacked, George sloped off to the centre of town, saying that he had errands to run and family to see. He was gone for three whole days during which I stayed at the hostel with no food: I only drank the brownish coloured water from the tap in my bathroom. The hostel didn't have a restaurant, and I didn't venture further than the end of the street, for fear of getting lost. In any case, I had no money in my pockets and didn't know how I would eat without being able to pay or to speak English. I stayed confined to my room. It was as big as a tomb and about as jolly. When I pushed the door open, I stumbled over my suitcase and fell on to the bed. Six or seven times a day I would say to myself "You can't stay here" and would go out of the hostel. I could see this flood of humanity being disgorged from the tube station exit and, not feeling able to go any further, I gave up, cursing George loudly and frequently under my breath.

After three days he re-appeared, visibly very happy with his stay in London. He must have been all-consumed by his shopping. Without any preamble, he said to me: "Hurry up, you're playing your first match in two hours!" I went to pieces. I hadn't eaten for three days; I clearly hadn't trained, and I had to play my first match in a grand slam tournament without having put a foot on the surface which was new to me. I also learnt quite soon that my opponent wasn't just anybody.

He was called Billy Martin, and I learnt later that he was the world's number one junior at the time. For those who knew about these things he was regarded as a future Rod Laver. Nevertheless, despite everything, I had high hopes of being able to beat him, especially when I saw time slipping by without him turning up. If he were to arrive more than a quarter of an hour after the due start-time, I would win by default. After ten minutes he had not shown up, and I was ready to relish my first grand slam win. If I'm honest I suspected it might be my only chance of getting through this first round and of getting a day's practice before the second round. Alas, two minutes before the fateful time he arrived, looking very self-confident, dressed immaculately and carrying a dozen Wilson rackets, whilst I hardly dare take my two out as they were very much the worse for wear. In the event I was hammered. At 6 – 0, 5 – 0 down, I heard George, my supposed companion, attempt a "Go on, Mansour, that's good, keep it up." At that point I couldn't contain myself, and I blew up. "You want me to keep what up, exactly? To end up with two love sets so that you can go home? Do you give a damn about me or what? In half a minute I will have lost six love, six love, and you'll tell me to "Keep it up"! Are you really barmy or are you doing it on purpose?"

Indeed, another thirty seconds later and it was all over. I was gutted. I felt that with a bit of practice and two meals a day I could have taken on Martin, certainly not to beat him but at least to make it a real match. It has to be said that Billy Martin didn't get much further in his career. That year he won Junior Wimbledon without losing more than three games in a match. Strangely, he never fulfilled his promise. He played his best tennis at that time but didn't break into the ranks of the great. I think his best ranking was as number 45 in the world. As a new Rod Laver, that's pretty modest ....

After this tragi-comic episode in England, life became serious. First, there was the Galea Cup – a competition reserved for players under twenty-one – held in 1975 in Czechoslovakia, one of the strongholds of world tennis. We had achieved an incredible run, knocking out Holland, Romania, Switzerland and France, one after the other; and now we were to come up against Czechoslovakia in the final. For the first time in my life I observed that strange look reserved for someone who has pulled off something great, that look that says: "I'd love to be in your position." I read all that in the glances that came in my direction. And it felt good. I didn't know exactly what it meant, but I felt it was delicious, intoxicating and, at the same time, very dangerous. At the end of the tournament the organisers came to ask me to stay on for two days after the conclusion, to play a local star too old to play in the Galea competition: Pavel Slozil. Naturally, I accepted. I asked for nothing more than to extend the blissful time, even by forty-eight hours. So I played Pavel Slozil: and I won. What a treat. I felt as if I were king of the world. Even the disagreeable remarks from the French players we had beaten were forgotten. Even so, it had rattled me when we were informed, without warning, of the comments of Christophe Roger-Vasselin who had said, after his defeat "These Iranians are cheats. They're at least thirty, not nineteen as they claim to be. Look at the one called Bahrami. He's a junior with the moustache of a forty-year-old. And it just so happens he's the strongest in their squad...." For them it had been a disaster to have been beaten by Iran. They couldn't understand how it was possible. Just imagine! France beaten by Iran at tennis! There had to be something fishy going on. Well, the fishy thing must have been my moustache....

I had had a moustache from the age of seventeen, when I became a man.

In Manila in 1974. The whole Iranian team.

Chapter Eight

DRAMA

In the holy city of Mashhad, on the pilgrimage with my parents.

I was seventeen, almost eighteen, already self-supporting and enjoying the notoriety of being a local champion. I was a young star, and life was made much easier with everything else which notoriety brought in its wake: girls, gifts, respect. What I appreciated most, however, was the pride I could see in the eyes of my parents. Ever since I had been really small, as I've mentioned, I had got into the habit of bringing money home, and now I was earning much more than my father: so there was no question but that I would make life easier for them too. But the first time I wanted to offer them a wad of notes, I found I couldn't do it. I could never have given it to my father. It would have constituted a terrible lack of respect for him and would have been worse even than to spit in his face; I went to my mother, therefore, feeling happy at the thought of the gift I was bringing. She refused it with a smile: "You know, Mansour, all the money you have given me since you were a small boy, all that money you earned selling bread rolls at the stadium and picking up balls on the courts, well, I didn't spend it. I put it in the bank." She handed me a deposit account book that showed it held the equivalent of about three thousand pounds! It was what I had earned over a dozen years of occasional work. She hadn't spent any of it, even in the worst of times, even when my father was straining every ounce of his strength to repay the loan taken out to buy the house. I wept, not really for joy, nor even from pain. It was just pure emotion, the kind you feel only with your parents or your children.

Since that amazing day, my mother hasn't accepted a penny from me, although she has from time to time asked me to help cousins or more distant relations. She didn't ever want anything for herself.

I decided that this money she had handed back to me should come to my parents in one way or another. They were both very devout, so I hit on the idea of funding their pilgrimage to Mecca, the *hajj* which all good muslims should carry out before their deaths. But it would have been almost an insult to offer to pay. The trip should be the result of a real financial effort on the part of the pilgrim. I opted for a much less demanding destination, therefore, in the form of the holy city of Mashhad in eastern Iran, where the tomb of the Imam

Reza, eighth most important in our religion, is located. It's one of Islam's most important sites.

As they had never travelled in an aeroplane before, I decided to go with them. When I recall their reactions at the airport, I can't help laughing. My father walked in front, and I followed with my mother a few steps behind. She wanted to know about everything she saw and bombarded me with questions about the airport, the planes, the armed guards …. I wasn't paying attention to what my father was doing until I heard him shouting and showing his anger against someone.

"Don't touch me. Who do you think you are? What do you want with me anyway?" He had arrived at the security area and was refusing to be searched. He was really angry; I don't think I have ever seen him so livid. I had to deploy whatever diplomatic skills I had to persuade the security people not to take him off in handcuffs, and it was even more difficult to get him to allow them to search him. "What do they think I'm hiding anyway? Do they think I'm a thief? I just won't stand for it!" I explained to him all about hijacks which had at that time only just begun to happen in the Middle East. I told him that no-one was taking him for a thief but that the security men needed to check that he wasn't armed, that they were under orders to frisk everybody for the same reason, that it was their job and that they couldn't make an exception, even for him. He finally agreed, but couldn't resist giving the guard an earful once the search was over: "Well then! You found the weapon I was concealing? Idiot! Imbecile!"

This pilgrimage turned out to be an overwhelming experience in my life. Apart from the pleasure of making the journey with my parents, I was moved to tears by what was unfolding in this place. I have explained already that I am not particularly affected by religion, but one cannot be indifferent to the fervour of those who live in these holy places. Years later I was to go to the Vatican and to Mecca, and I found exactly the same internal fire as I did at Mashhad. It was very serene, a feeling of being nothing and yet everything. I know that sounds a bit confused, but those readers who have spent time in places of this kind will understand.

This gift to my parents had made me proud and self-confident. Seeing them smiling at me throughout this excursion made me feel I had become a responsible adult. It was as if my father had passed me the baton while I led him into one of Islam's holy cities.

I'm not sure if this feeling of responsibility changed me radically, but the events which followed propelled me into a world that was new for me.

For it was around this time that I met Sabri. She was one of the most beautiful girls in Tehran. All the men looked at her with a mixture of desire and fear. People didn't dare go up to talk to her because her beauty was so intimidating. If she felt anyone might not be able to please her, she had a way of freezing them out before they dared to say anything. Her father was an important general, chief of the air staff and someone close to the Shah, which added to her status as an unapproachable woman. And she was the one who had picked me up....

From the time when I had become a professional tennis player, I hardly ever played at Amjadieh any more. Instead I would go to the Imperial Country Club. This was the smartest tennis club in Iran, a place where the regime's most important personalities would meet up. My two sponsoring godfathers had introduced me there and, quite quickly, my status as a local star had been established. I often noticed Sabri there but, like the other young men of my age, didn't dare chat her up, and even found it difficult to look straight at her. On this particular day she came right up to me, smiling, and suggested going to the open-air cinema together. I turned her down, because she frightened me and I couldn't imagine taking her out anywhere. She insisted however, and that same evening found us sitting together watching some Hollywood production. It was she who took the lead, even caressing my little finger with hers before taking my hand. Our first kiss lasted for hours! I just fell in love with her. I had made love to other girls before her, which was made easier by my reputation as an accomplished sportsman and experienced traveller, but I had never loved a woman, a real woman. Sabri became my first love.

At the club she insisted that we kiss in public, because she liked provoking a reaction, and that certainly succeeded. Many were those who looked at us askance and those who stared at us head on; firstly because public embraces were simply not done, above all at the Imperial Country Club and certainly not when a general's daughter was messing with a gardener's son, even if he was a tennis champion. I could feel malevolent looks burrowing into my back and was always conscious of the gap in our social status. She didn't consider that at all important. I loved her, she loved me, and the rest meant nothing to her. My friends told me I was crazy to be seen around with her, that some day or another her father would get to hear about it and that I would end my days in the desert with a bullet in the back of my head. They meant it, and I have to admit that their warnings did frighten me. But I was in love, and my fears made Sabri laugh. She was a year or so older than me; she had been at school in London, knew exactly how to behave and could speak foreign languages. She had that rebellious side you sometimes find in rich kids who have had the opportunity to look beyond the gates of their glorious ghettos. She seemed at ease everywhere, with my friends and family as much as in her privileged world. Beyond the frosty barrier she had erected despite herself, she was charming, sweet, generous and likeable. But even though she felt at home wherever she went, the same was not true for me. She brought me into her social life where I felt like an alien. With her I rubbed shoulders with high society and came across the same people as at the club. I found no problem on the tennis court but did feel out of place as soon as I stepped into their world. Some of them showed themselves to be sympathetic towards me, others not. No-one told me openly that I didn't belong in these circles, but some made it obvious in their expressions or by leaving when I arrived .... If truth be told, it was I who shut myself out. Fixed in my mind were the awareness of my social background and the certainty that it could never be compatible with the luxury of their world. Sabri did everything she could to avoid my being embarrassed, but I couldn't make the adjustment. Only the love I swore to her and above all the sublime pleasure I felt at being with her prevented me from running away from it all. It's a stupid fact that the biggest gulf between her friends and me was a matter of clothes. I simply didn't have the same garb as them, no Italian suits or American jeans. I remember a party to which I went with her, in one of those sumptuous homes you would find in the north of Tehran where the Shah's coterie lived. It was a themed event, and the men had to dress in the style of Chicago in the nineteen-twenties. They all looked like Al Capone, and I, in an over-large suit lent to me by Shirzad Akbari, must have looked like a clown. The sneaky smiles grew broader, and I felt more and more humiliated. The demonstrative kisses which Sabri gave me might have made the other men jealous, but they didn't bring back a smile to my face.

Eventually we left, went away and made love. Then I forgot completely the humiliation and rage which I had felt. We continued on the same path for several months more, and I think it would have lasted a lifetime, if a certain drama had not intervened.

She had left for a few days' skiing. I stayed in Tehran to continue training. An aneurismal rupture floored her when she arrived at the end of her last descent, on the last day of her holidays. She was dying, but her father chartered a plane specially to take her to a private clinic in Switzerland. I had no news at all for more than a month. I was in a deep pit, believing that she had died and that no-one dared tell me. She was alive, however, but paralysed. Her brain had suffered irreversible damage, and she had no control over the left-hand side of her body.

When I finally got news of what had happened to my darling Sabri, it was three months since I had seen her. I tried to trace her, without knowing whether she had stayed in Switzerland or was being treated elsewhere. I had made up my mind to go and see her father, despite being terrified of him. Several months after Sabri's accident, however, her father died in a hang-gliding accident.

Eventually, I saw her fifteen years later. She was living in England and had seen the poster for a tournament in which I was playing. She was waiting for me at the exit from the court on which I had been playing against Wojtek Fibak. Recognising her instantly, I fell into her arms. We were weeping helplessly.

At the Imperial Country Club in Tehran, in 1977, with
Chouchou and Fatimah.

Chapter Nine

DREAMED LIFE

After Sabri, my life resumed. I went out with girls, as I had done before meeting her, but I couldn't fall in love. I just wanted to concentrate on playing tennis. My career took on a new momentum, which was just as well.

My success in the Galea Cup, in Czechoslovakia, had convinced my godfathers that I ought to move into top gear. They decided that my adult singles career should begin straightaway, at the Stockholm tournament, in December 1976. There was snow three feet deep in the streets. That's about all I can remember. I lost in the second round of the qualification stage, and I left to go into training in Florida.

It was fabulous. The weather was beautiful, I was with other Iranian players.... We trained for about a fortnight before setting off across the southern states to compete in some small tournaments. We were a good group: there was a Romanian whose first name was Gabriel: he was a real character. He had used a trip to Belgium, thanks to the Galea Cup competition, to slip away into the West. Thereafter his main aim was to sleep with as many girls as possible. He was continually on antibiotics because, at the time, people didn't take so many precautions, and venereal diseases were rife. I had a great time with him. I had also become quite a skirt-chaser myself but, alongside Gabriel, I must have seemed like a monk. Whereas I notched up three conquests a week, he would reach the same score in a day! On the other hand, I had an unbeatable chat-up line to outscore him. When the girls asked where I came from and I replied "Iran", they would immediately hit the follow-up question: "But there's oil there, isn't there?" The red carpet unfurled in front of me, and I just needed to feign a distant-looking expression before saying: "Yes, there's quite a lot of oil. We have a few wells in our family." It worked every time.

Gabriel didn't need to adopt the role of rich scion of the family. He was so obsessed, so much on the pull, that he just needed to be himself, or to reel off the first story that came into his head, to have it away with the American girls.

Gabriel and me, in Florida, summer 1977.

The Iranian national team, in Florida, 1977.

We were living in the glorious days before AIDS but after the Pill, sexual liberation, the death of taboos and the end of restrictions. What a party....

One evening we had picked up two girls in a restaurant, in Jacksonville, Florida. They were called Debby and Linda. I fancied Linda a lot: she looked like Barbra Streisand, and we went out together for several weeks. I would go to play my tournaments in Florida, and every weekend she would come to join me, wherever I was playing. Her pal Debby went with her to be with Gabriel. Although my Linda adventure didn't last, Debby did stay with Gabriel. She also made a tremendous effort to make me take up again with Linda. According to her, Linda was in despair and was simply waiting for a sign from me. When she saw that her arguments weren't getting her anywhere, Debby ended up by pitching a strong one at me: "Linda is

pregnant, and she wants to keep the baby and settle down with you."
I didn't give in. To tell the truth, I didn't believe it.

When I returned to Jacksonville, twenty years later, to play in a
veterans' tournament, accompanied by my wife, I warned her not to
be astonished if a good-looking twenty-year-old, with a moustache
like mine were to come up to us and call me daddy....

Chapter Ten

THE EXTRA-TERRESTRIAL

The group of players with whom I went around weren't all party-goers and pick-up merchants. Apart from my great friend David Schneider, I saw a lot of Gene Meyer, Peter McNamara and Paul McNamee. These latter two were to go on to have outstanding careers and, as a doubles partnership, carry off several grand slam titles. They took tennis seriously, probably a bit more seriously than me; I was only beginning to discover the professional circuit, however that didn't prevent them from having a good time. On arrival at some place, we would hire a four or five-seat car so that we could tour around once we had been eliminated from the tournament, which happened usually after two or three days. We always went out as a group, which magnified enormously the quota of schoolboy humour. It was a good life, a wandering life, one week here, another week somewhere else, covering all the continents. And all this just to "play"! We had a juvenile mindset, a wonderful profession and financial means which, while not being out of this world, allowed us still to have a good time. We were often more than fifteen or twenty in a restaurant, with eight or nine nationalities around the table. At first I couldn't understand anything anyone said to me, but then, thanks to hanging out with South Africans, Australians and Americans, I got the hang of English. In any case we had very few philosophical discussions; and, larking about, as we did, a degree in foreign languages was not required.

One of my close friends was a French player who unfortunately has since committed suicide; I got to know Pascal Deniau in Sweden at a small tournament. On the final day we had gone shopping and, in the underground railway, he showed me what he had bought, including a pair of Eminence underpants. I had never seen anything so classy, and as I had to leave the following day to return to Tehran, I offered him double what he had paid for them. He refused, and when he hadn't given in, after ten minutes of bartering, with a casual look on my face I nicked them from him. When he got out of the train and the doors had closed, I tapped on the glass and held up the pants for him to see. I thought it was hilarious. He just couldn't believe it. He chased after the train, which of course got him nowhere. I expected to see him a few weeks later, but the events in Iran meant that we didn't meet up until five years later, in 1981, at a tournament in Lille. As soon as he saw me, in the clubhouse which was teeming with people, he started joking and asking what I had done with his pants. Believe it or not, I was wearing them! I offered to give them back to him there and then. Fortunately for me, he took a charitable line.

Some great players looked at me strangely because I said hello to everyone and therefore to them as well. I could feel them wondering: "Who is that, anyway?"

I didn't have the same attitude as them. I tried to be friendly with everyone, didn't consider myself to be out-of-the-ordinary and didn't adopt the disdainful attitude of quite a few of the players. In that respect, I didn't fit in with the élite of the tennis world. I was spontaneous, and when I met a great tennis player I looked at him awestruck. I was proud to be moving in the same circles as him. It's not in my nature to pretend I wasn't impressed. Then there were always those "hellos" that I used when I met someone I knew for the first time that day. For me it was natural but, with hindsight, I understand that most of these lads asked themselves: "Who is this pain in the neck?"

It was by playing backgammon that I found I fitted in best. I threw dice with Nastase, Connors and some other great players. I have to admit that I was a last resort invitee to the table, when they had found no-one else available. But that wasn't because of my non-ranked status but because I beat them every time! It would be a great end to the month for me and it allowed me to meet people, to form friendships rather than staying on my own in a corner. The snag was that, very soon, Ilie Nastase fouled everything up for me. As soon as he saw anyone offering to play me, he would shout: "You're crazy! You mustn't play dice with that Iranian; he's too strong, and he'll thrash you!" I didn't dare interrupt to shut him up. I saw Nastase as a genius and found him inspirational. I loved his game, and he was at his peak then. I was a nobody, and I reckoned I was just lucky to be able to roll the dice with him. I allowed him to rain on my parade, knowing that he would want me to be available, above all, to play against him. Quickly my reputation got around the small world of the tennis tour, and the players became wary of me. But, also, they became my friends ....

As I mentioned, I was spending a lot of time with David Schneider, a South African who played for Israel in the Davis Cup. He was then, and still is, one of the best friends of Jimmy Connors. David is still a good friend of mine too; but our first meeting didn't augur well for a lasting friendship. I had asked him two or three times if he wanted to practise with me; and he hardly said anything in reply. Then, after the start of a tournament in Durban, he proposed going to knock a few balls around. So we went off, and after a couple of minutes he was hitting balls all over the place, at random, saying that they were too light. After five minutes he was so upset he left the court. I thought: "What an idiot this guy is, and how disrespectful." Before leaving the court he asked, aggressively: "Do you play backgammon? You want to have a game?" I said yes. He started bragging, saying he only played for money – ten dollars a point. I accepted. An hour later he owed me six hundred and twenty dollars and started tearing his hair out. But he didn't want to call a halt there. I decided to tell him the truth: "I'm much too strong a player for you. You hardly know how to play, and what's more, the way you're stressed out, you're completely reckless in the way you're playing. You'll owe me six thousand dollars after a couple of hours and will go bust." But he was really obstinate, and I didn't know what to do to stop the massacre. In the end, he was in such a mess I reduced his losses to twenty dollars. All he was prepared to do was to buy me a beer. Despite all this, we became good mates.

With Jimmy Connors, Bill Lelly and David Schneider, during a dinner at my home in Paris, 1992.

I enjoyed growing up on this professional tennis circuit. I felt perfectly at ease but, as I have hinted, I was really out of synch with most of my colleagues. I think sometimes I must have come across as an extraterrestrial being. I made an even bigger number of gaffes by being so uninhibited. I made everyone smile, sometimes unintentionally ....

It was 1976. We were playing at a moderately important tournament in Khartoum in Sudan. I had lost in the third round and was practising while waiting to move on to Cairo for the next tournament. Every day representatives of the ATP (the Association of Tennis Professionals which organise the tournaments) were asking me in English if I had had my yellow fever shot. I didn't really understand what they were asking me but, eventually, I realised that it had something to do with vaccinations; and, as my vaccination booklet was yellow, I assumed they were asking me if I had my booklet with me. I must have assumed that "fever" meant "folder". So I carried on saying yes. I could feel, nevertheless, that they weren't entirely convinced and began to wonder why ....

Arriving in Cairo on the last flight from Khartoum, around eleven at night, I didn't feel at all worried. The players were passing through customs and immigration, showing their passports and vaccination booklets. The official checking the validity of the documents immediately signalled to them to go through. I brandished my *yellow fever* at him, expecting to be able to carry on through. I heard him say: "Please stop!" The chap in uniform was saying to me: "You don't have the yellow fever shot;" I showed him my booklet saying "This is my yellow fever." I decided that this chap was a complete idiot. The misunderstanding lasted for three or four minutes during which I was saying: "This is yellow, isn't it?" showing him my booklet. He answered with an air of incredulity: "Yes, the booklet is yellow, but you haven't been vaccinated against yellow fever!" Eventually the other players and an ATP official intervened in this surreal conversation and made me realise that this man was not the cretin I had taken him for.

I confess I was a bit ashamed to have misunderstood the situation so disastrously. Soon, shame was replaced by anxiety. Once again, I had got off to a bad start.

There was nothing to be done, no preferential treatment to be hoped for. No vaccination, no entry to Egypt. The official was dogmatic: either I turned round and took the first flight out or I would be sent into quarantine for a week. I wasn't too keen on a week locked up in Cairo, but the next plane back took off at the end of the morning. When I asked what quarantine consisted of, the official replied: "It's a five star hotel, and you get free board and lodging." And I believed him ....

An army jeep drove me two or three kilometres from the airport, right out into the desert, to a one-storey building surrounded by a six-foot fence and guarded by an armed soldier. They took away my passport and took me to my room. If indeed you could call it a room. The walls were sweating with humidity, the mattress was stained with mildew and the sheets were soaked through. It was as cold as a dungeon, and I took all the clothes out of my bag to try to sleep on the floor, with my head on my knees. In the morning, the flies chased away the mosquitoes, and drought arrived in place of the coldness of the night. I was right out in the desert, in a medical isolation centre, in Egypt, at the end of the nineteen-seventies. I'm sure you get the picture. There were six of us in this place, five Nigerians and me. I couldn't stop thinking of the chap at the airport who must have told the story to all his mates of how he made a benighted Iranian tennis player believe he would be spending a week's quarantine in a five-star hotel. That made me mad, and I turned round and round, hurling insults at the flies. By nightfall, the same story all over again, freezing cold and sleeping on the ground, wrapped in my three outer garments.

After two nights of this, I demanded to speak to the Iranian Embassy. The ambassador was called…. Bahrami. I thought I saw a signal and convinced myself that I would get out because he was going to get on the case. He did the latter: a secretary brought me a kilo of oranges, saying that he couldn't do anything else for me. I ate nothing but those oranges for two days, and then I cracked. I decided to break out. I watched the guard armed with a machine gun; he was rather scrawny, and I was sure that he wouldn't offer any resistance if he saw me making a run for it. If needs be, a little smack would have floored him. So I took the opportunity, clambered over the fence and jumped down on the other side. I could see the guard looking at me with a mocking expression. I even felt that he was laughing at me, and that was a bit disconcerting. I started walking and realised that I was alone, on foot, without a passport, in the Egyptian desert. Where was I going to go? How was I going to get out of the country, without my passport, any money or an airline ticket? They had confiscated everything. So I turned round. When I passed in front of the guard, he stopped laughing and looked at my head. That was what stopped him receiving a clip round the ear.

The next day, Richard Evans, the ATP supervisor, came to rescue me. He had got – I don't know how – papers from highly-placed people demanding my immediate release. The guards asked for some bakshish for the return of my passport, and so I got out my wad of bank-notes. They took practically all my money. The rest was pinched by the taxi driver who drove me to the Al-Ghazira Tennis Club, venue for the tournament in which I was due to play. I didn't put up any resistance as I was so happy to be back in the world.

In the lounge reserved for the players all my colleagues gathered round me to listen to the latest adventure of Mr Bahrami, the extraterrestrial of the tennis tour. I said: "Well, O.K., but show me where the restaurant is!" I ate enough for four people and couldn't get up from my chair for more than an hour.

The next week, at Alexandria, I won the doubles tournament, partnered by Jacques Thamin, playing against Hutka and Simbera, who at that time were Czechoslovakia's Davis Cup pairing.

Despite the incidents along the way, all was turning out for the best in my world. My game was getting stronger, and I felt more at ease among my colleagues. I have to admit, too, that I confirmed time and time again their perception of my gullibility.

Tommy Krice, an American player, had always beaten me 6-0, 6-0 in training. One day in Florence, the day before a tournament, he arrived, panic-stricken, on the court where I was knocking up with my friend David Schneider. He was shattered and began talking to me as if he were going to break the news of the death of someone close to him: "Mansour, I've got bad news for you: the draw has been posted, and you're going to lose in the first round because you are up against me." He was serious, not bluffing. First of all, I took it in a joking way, saying that it didn't matter, but he stuck to his line, saying: "Really, it's too much for you, and for me it's worrying, because I like

you, and you'll be out at the first stage. To be frank, it's not fair...."
He wound me up with his commiserating in advance of the event,
and I reminded him that to lose in practice games was one thing, to
lose in competition, something else. Certainly for me. That calmed
him down for a bit. But an hour later he came back, this time all
smiles. "Mansour, Mansour, they're going to revise the draw, because
there has been a mistake with the entries. It's brilliant, because we're
not going to play each other." I went on practising. He went off, but
ten minutes later he was back: "It's unbelievable, they've re-done the
draw again, and we're back playing against each other. You could say
that you're just unlucky, Mansour. You can't imagine how that upsets
me." I chose to ignore him.

The next day, I won the first set of our match easily and managed
to get a break of serve game in the second. Tommy was distraught,
almost in tears. So I began to say to myself: "Be a nice person, Mansour,
what does it mean to you, to win this match? Look at this poor chap;
it's as if he's going to have an arm torn off if you win this match. He's
a good mate, you're sharing a room in the hotel. Go on, let him play,
you just can't let him lose, it would really hurt him, whereas you don't
give a damn...." I began to drop points deliberately, letting him take
points, holding out the offer of winning. He won the second set. At
the start of the third set, I began to understand; every time he won a
point he bawled, clenched his fist and stared at me malevolently, as
if he wanted to defy me, bury me. He didn't even realise that he was
still on the court because I had decided not to compete at full stretch.
That upset me a lot. He was leading three games to one in the final
set, and I wondered why he wasn't as sorry for me as I had been for
him while he was losing. I realised I was being a cretin, confusing
friendship and competition. I began to play seriously again and won
the match without dropping another game. He was crushed. He left
the court at top speed, completely deflated. When I saw him next,
he was phoning California, speaking to his father who paid his travel
expenses. I heard him say that the tour was just too difficult, that he
had lost a match in the opening round again by coming up against a
real hot-shot, and that he felt like throwing in the towel and coming
home. His father probably asked who it was that he had come up

against, and Tommy answered: "Against John Yul!" Now John Yul was a good friend, a South African of about the same age as us and who was thrashing everyone around this time. After he had hung up Tommy said to me sheepishly: "Mansour, forgive me, but if I had told him I had lost to a certain Iranian player called Bahrami, I think my father would have thrown some insults at me and told me not to come home. I didn't have any choice …." I found that so extreme I wasn't even annoyed.

Chapter Eleven

HAPPY DAYS IN TEHRAN

That was how 1976 was played out, with happy times on the tour as well as in Tehran. I was overjoyed, I had converted my dream into reality. I was having a good time, my tennis was improving, and I was earning enough to live on comfortably, mainly thanks to my sponsors. But not just thanks to them. I was achieving some good results in minor tournaments, and that allowed me to put a little money aside. That, however, wasn't in my nature either. In earlier years, in fact, as soon as I had money in my pocket, I had gone to play in the casino. I could have three thousand dollars, or its equivalent in Iranian tumans, one day, and lose it all the next. At the casino in Tehran I never won a penny. As I didn't have a bank account at the time, all my money was in my pocket. It was a treat for the croupiers....

I was living like that, from day to day, in a small flat rented with a friend. Fortunately, when I started to rub shoulders with professionals on the ATP tour, I got myself organised and stopped doing just anything I fancied. I didn't become an ant, but I did succeed in dampening my grasshopper spirit. Therefore, when my old childhood hero, Shirzad Akbari, suggested buying a superb piece of ground on which we could build a house for us both, I already had the equivalent of the thirty thousand pounds needed to complete the purchase. This was at the beginning of 1977. I remember the pride I felt when he came and suggested the collaboration. Shirzad, my idol, the one who had given me my first serious racket. His idea that we become neighbours filled me with pride. It was like a sign of gratitude. An architect friend kindly drew up the plans for the house. The intention was that Shirzad would occupy the ground floor, and I the upper floor. Our budget was fairly tight and the plans ambitious, so we couldn't afford for everything to be done by the construction workers. So we became tennis-player builders for a few months. I enhanced my physique by navvying with sacks of sand and cement. My muscle tone was improved man-handling bricks. Truth be told, my tennis service was stronger after that ....

It took us almost a year to make our "palace" rise from the ground. Naturally, I wasn't working on this full-time, as I had to leave often to compete in tennis tournaments abroad. I was leading a double life; builder for one week a month, tennis professional for the rest of the time – a nice balance.

My house. At the age of twenty-two I had my own big, beautiful house, whilst my father had had to wait until he was almost seventy to own his.

In our new home there were always plenty of people, our respective girlfriends and pals who had arrived to have a drink or to play dice. It was a bit like the TV soap operas which are popular nowadays. We were acting out "Friends" in Tehran, a few months before the Islamic Revolution!

At the time, I felt that a wind of freedom was blowing across Tehran. I suppose it wasn't the same for all Iranians, but for me, that's how I was living: I went to the casino, partied, spent whole nights in discotheques. At this same time, those who wanted to live strictly in accordance with their religion could do that: nothing prevented them. The city was expanding at an extraordinary rate, and it was getting more westernised day by day. Modern technology and architecture were becoming the norm. Businessmen were making a lot of money, and many places dedicated to parting these well-to-do people from their money were opening up. The young women were more liberated than ever before. Alcohol flowed freely; and many artists, musicians, actors and poets were flexing their creative muscles. Tehran was far from being New York of the nineteen-eighties, but a powerful, festive, cultural and liberal breeze was making itself felt.

There's no question of my making excuses for the regime of the Shah – the memories of my youth bear witness to the life of the poor not being easy – but I have to say that there was considerable freedom in everyday life. This freedom was completely obliterated by the Revolution.

To the best of my recollection, despite difficulties in his life, I never heard my father criticise the Shah. On the contrary, he spoke of the royal family with great respect and would often tell me that Iran was "a country where bandits could cut your throat at any moment before the time when the Pahlavis came to power." My father was a devout Muslim, but he never supported the Islamic Revolution. He was a traditionalist and considered the Shah was leading the country for the best. Nevertheless, the behaviour of the regime's inner circle, towards the end of the Shah's reign, was abhorrent in many ways.

In Tehran, 1976, with Ezat Nematy. Meeting the Shah of Iran during the Aryamehr Cup event

An ATP tournament had been arranged for a long time: it was the Aryamehr Cup, i.e. the Cup in honour of his Excellency the

King, and had attracted some of the best players in the world. I had taken part for several years but, in 1977, I harboured new ambitions. My status as a young local hopeful wasn't enough: I wanted to shine in front of my people.

In the opening round I beat Omar Laimina; in the second round I was due to play the South African Bob Hewitt at 3.00 p.m. on the Wednesday. The centre court was packed, I had begun to develop a popular following in Tehran, and the crowd expected something from me. Half an hour before the start of the match I was waiting in the dressing-room, wondering why my opponent had still not arrived. Five minutes before the start, when I was in the corridor leading on to the court, and as I looked at the crammed terraces and listened to the crowd shouting my name, the Federation secretary came up to me and said: "Mansour, you're not playing today. Your opponent is ill, and we don't want him to be knocked out by default. He is well-known, and for the prestige of the tournament, it would be better to postpone the match. He's going to rest all day, and you can play him tomorrow. It's important you don't tell anyone: we're going to find a reason for his not being here...." My first thought was that this was a joke, but then I didn't go along with the idea. "It's against all the rules," I said, "I'm going to see the ATP supervisor. If Hewitt doesn't play me now, he's forfeited the match, and I've qualified for the quarter-finals."

The secretary left without saying a word. The journalists leapt on to the case, as if they could smell something fishy. At the time, there were all kinds of pretexts for criticising the regime, and they asked me what was going on. I had just begun to explain to them when the tournament director stormed in, throwing them out of the dressing-room and saying: "You're making a big mistake, Mansour. There's no point in talking to the journalists. Your opponent won't be eliminated. If you want to play, you'll play tomorrow and, whatever the result, you'll be paid as if you had won. I'll be frank with you, anyway: you can do whatever you want, we don't care. There's no way Bob Hewitt is going to be knocked out today."

I felt deflated, angry and frustrated. But I knew these mediocre little officials quite well. They wouldn't relent and, if I alerted the ATP, it would be the supervisor who would have problems with them. I swallowed my frustration and controlled my rage. That night I didn't sleep but drank whisky as the anger turned over in my head. The next day I was a zombie on the court, had no wish to play and so gave in, played without purpose and, despite my lacklustre performance, got beaten by only 6 − 4, 6 − 4.

Upon reflection, I held it against myself terribly that I hadn't had the opposite reaction, not to have gone all-out for winning and to have undermined those who had tried to stop me playing. If I had won, they would have told everyone that they were the reason for my breakthrough. If I lost, that was also O.K., because there was no risk they would have been put in the shade. I was beginning to get well known, and my little bit of notoriety frightened them. How could this be? A player was set to be famous, putting the officials into the shade? It may seem incredible, but in Iran, at that time, sportsmen had to be good enough for the sport to survive, but not so good as to become heroes.

Heroes are dangerous. As a popular figure I could have exposed what had happened to me as a child and could have evaded the iniquitous decisions of low-level officials. I should have qualified by right for the quarter-finals of the King's Cup in 1977. Instead of that I took my money, went home and got sloshed. I sickened myself and was sickened by the mind-set of a certain marginal group of Iranians.

None of us were to know it, but the King's Cup had had its last year. The following year, the students were on the streets, and the revolution was sweeping all before it ….

I knew that the country was in a bad way and that it was going to end dramatically. How to explain that?

I'm not sure, but in Tehran there was a kind of excess of madness among the party-goers, more of a reproachful attitude from those used to living modestly. Ways of behaving became more extreme. It was as if one lived at a greater speed because one could feel that everything might come to a halt soon. Tehran changed gear, its tempo accelerated and peoples' wildness seemed to increase. I was in Switzerland when I heard that the catastrophe was imminent.

At the beginning of 1978, an Iranian team was competing against a Swiss team in the Davis Cup competition at the Eaux-Vives Park in Geneva. Because of the tense situation in the country, for several weeks the Iranian authorities had delayed sending the team, in which I was the number one player. Right up to the day before, we were not sure we would set off. On arrival, therefore, I decided that we wouldn't have made the journey in vain. We had to beat the Swiss, led by Heinz Günthart, even though they were clear favourites.

In Paris, with Farah Diba and Christian Bîmes, president of the French Tennis Federation. Her Majesty is a great tennis fan and an excellent player.

I won my singles match to bring the score to one match each by the Friday night. The next day, when we arrived on court to practise for the doubles, the clay court surface was as hard as concrete, and there was what looked like a huge dark stain in the middle of the court. We were told that, during the night, students hostile to the Shah's regime had poured several barrels of oil on to the court, to prevent the fixture going ahead. The staff at Eaux-Vives had tried to salvage the situation, but everyone was shocked at what had happened. I, above all, was shocked! It was at that moment that I realised that nothing would be as before when we got home.

Despite the oily surface, we won the doubles, and I went to visit some fellow-countrymen in Geneva's finest hotel, La Réserve. The hotel manager came to greet me and said: "I saw you playing yesterday in the singles and just now in the doubles. I like your style. If you need work some day, come here and you can become La Réserve's tennis pro'. That will earn you three or four thousand dollars a month, and you can get to know the upper crust of Geneva, which might be useful." I thanked him and forgot about it ....

On the Sunday, the Swiss made the score two matches all, and my duel with Heinz Günthart was to be the decider. I played ten match points against this player who later went on to be Steffi Graf's coach. My spirit was absent, and I lost ....

Chapter Twelve

THE ASSASSINATION

We returned, defeated, to Tehran, but nobody cared. We above all. It was clear to everyone that the Iranian people didn't want the monarchy any more, that people had turned against inequality and that the mass of the population didn't know exactly what they wanted, but they were sure they wanted something different. It didn't matter, really, who or what would run the country, the population didn't want the Shah, and that was enough of a reason to bring on the revolution. After that, we'd see what happened ....

I trained with the other Iranian players despite the worsening situation, working like convicts aiming to pull off a master coup – which, we realised, would be our last great coup – at the King's Cup which was due to take place the following October. But, a fortnight after our return from Geneva, it was already over. We realised the King's Cup would never take place. Organising it was dangerous, and bringing in players from abroad was too much of a risk for the government. It is true that, at a time when people were demonstrating in the street against wretched living conditions, it would have been obscene to pay out a hundred and fifty thousand dollars to tennis players. The organisers thought that hordes of misery merchants would attack the players, crying out "We're starving!" They feared a massacre, and I suppose they weren't wrong. Also, who were going to be the spectators? Who, in those troubled times, was going to sit in the stands watching tennis?

Already by October 1978 many rich families were leaving Iran. Our sponsors left, taking their moveable assets with them. The tennis club was deserted. In the space of six months, everything had changed, and Tehran wasn't the same city as before.

One day, wandering along the streets I knew so well, I heard the clamour of the crowd before I noticed hundreds of running armed policemen. I went on for another few yards or so to get round the corner of the street and then saw thousands of people demonstrating for the removal of the Shah. There was a clash and many killed, but I had already turned on my heels and headed for home.

I didn't go out again for several weeks, except for some visits to my parents and essential errands to some of the few shopkeepers still open. I avoided the centre of town and didn't go into bars or restaurants. In any case, they had all drawn down their shutters.

Tehran was on fire. From my home I could see the plumes of smoke coming up from the centre of town. I went with three of my friends one morning to see the situation at first-hand. We went along the wide Takhte-Jamshid Avenue in my car. Some buildings were burnt out, others still burning. Shops had been pillaged, their shutters distorted and windows broken. Looters were everywhere; it was chaotic, as if a cataclysmic earthquake had struck.

I stopped the car alongside the pavement, not sure if I should turn round or go on. We saw, on the other side of the avenue, two street-kids who were walking in our direction, twenty yards away. No doubt they were on the prowl for some food or the chance to force an entry into a shop to steal some provisions.

They were too late in hearing the sound of an army jeep coming up behind them. When it stopped opposite them, they crouched in the porch of a doorway just in front of us, perhaps ten yards away. A soldier hardly any older than them got out of the jeep and started shouting at them. He began beating them with his rifle-butt. The kids covered their heads as best they could with their arms. Then one of them made a break for it. He dodged out of the way underneath the rifle-butt and began to run. The soldier didn't put his rifle to his shoulder. He raised his weapon to hip-level and shot twice into the back of the youngster. It was almost at point-blank range. The boy did a kind of pirouette, a precarious leap and fell on to the pavement. A pool of blood soon formed.

Still today I can picture that scene as if it had just happened. It's like a film image. But it's real. The soldier, just a boy himself, had lost his self-control and murdered a child. Just like that. And in front of me and my friends Hadi, Behrouz and Yadi. We couldn't utter a word or form the simplest of gestures.

The soldier snatched up the body of the boy and tossed it into the back of the jeep, like a sack of potatoes. I could see the expression of the other boy, eyes wide open, looking out at the scene without moving. His cries were silenced now. He was like a piece of statuary, stretched out, gazing at the pool of blood, all that remained of his little pal. The jeep drove off, and just as we were opening the doors of my car to go to help the other kid, other people arrived, alerted by the two gun-shots. They carried the boy away while some men dipped their hands into the pool of blood and showed their hands to the others. The crowd was now shouting and getting worked up. We left, traumatised by what we had seen, an assassination by the Shah's men in the middle of Tehran. It was one assassination among hundreds of others. And this was before the thousands which were to be perpetrated by the Islamic fundamentalists.

Within a few weeks the country was emptied of its greatest pots of personal wealth. The tennis club was still deserted. The courts were deteriorating at a staggering speed. Those who stayed, like me and quite a few others, didn't dare even to go to hit a ball around. Playing tennis during the revolution would inevitably have invited trouble. The extremists could always have beaten you up with an incantation that "it's immoral and anti-religious to play tennis while good Muslims are bringing the revolution." I was well aware that, in time, this was going to bring me big problems – I had to train regularly to be able to continue my profession – but I hardly had a choice, and had little prospect of an improvement in the situation. I would have to leave too, but getting a visa had become Mission Impossible. I knew that a clandestine exit was always conceivable, but those who took that route could never come back to Iran. I couldn't see myself abandoning family, friends and social circle. In effect, my whole life. No, I felt, I couldn't leave everything, even for tennis. So I came towards the end of 1978 without hitting a single ball. And it wasn't going to get any better in 1979.

In January 1979 the Islamic Republic was proclaimed, and the theoreticians of the regime declared that tennis was an imperialist, American and capitalist game. So they simply prohibited it. I didn't hit a ball again, therefore, until 1980.

I was convinced that this time my career was well and truly finished. I played dice games to avoid thinking about it, to brush away dark thoughts. And to make a living ....

We began around nine o'clock in the morning, and by the time we finished, eyes reddened and brains hazy, dawn was often breaking. You have to imagine what it was like, in this revolutionary period. The tedium was deadly, and no-one was being very ingenious any more to relieve it. The best ruse was to put your faith in failure and simply hope for better days. An all-pervasive uncertainty prevailed, as we didn't know if we would still be alive the next day: people were being strung up without anyone knowing really why. In conditions like that everyone can legitimately ask whether it will be your turn next. We avoided thinking about it too much by betting what little we had left. It was impossible to live normally. Everything was forbidden and dangerous. You had to queue to buy the simplest loaf of bread in the shops. As for alcohol, it was almost easier. Everybody knew a bootlegger who sold real American bourbon or scotch on the black market. You simply had to be discreet. If you were caught in possession of a bottle of alcohol you got a hundred lashes with a whip and a few days in prison. If you offended again, worse luck, you were imprisoned for life, at best. As for the bootlegger, the penalty was simpler: automatically he was hanged, after a show-trial staged by the religious authorities.

Between the days devoted to dice games I went to visit my parents, three or four times a week. I was anxious about my father who was not living well in retirement. He wanted to find some work. That now became an obsession with him, and it made him irritable and aggressive, above all with my mother who, as ever, accepted it without begrudging her unjust destiny. His mind turned it over and over, and one couldn't say anything to him without him flying into a rage. Often he would go off walking in the streets for the whole day. Sometimes he would spend some time in the mosque, to pray and see his friends. But that didn't satisfy him. He was driven by the work ethic, and that's what he missed. It's unbelievable, but it's true. He had worked like a slave all his life and now, when he could finally put his feet up, he had gone crazy.

I needed to work, too, but I was twenty-three! Rather than moping around we decided to enlist the support of all the tennis lovers we knew. We went to see the new minister of sport. We begged him to let us play, telling him that we were ordinary citizens, that we knew nothing about capitalism except the word because we were sons of workers and gardeners. Our oratory must have been effective; after a few more weeks of protestations and supplications we persuaded the authorities to let us organise a little tournament, the Revolutionary Cup. Of course the religious authorities forbade any foreigner to take part. But no-one would have been crazy enough to come and compete in a tennis tournament in Tehran in 1980 ....

We were dubious right up to the final moment. We felt sure the revolutionary committee would change its mind and that, even before the end of the first match, the revolutionary guards would pile in, give everyone a drubbing, stop the tournament and clap the players in irons. That's how it was in those days. Anything could happen. Especially the worst.

But, in the final analysis, I wasn't in a high risk category.

Professional tennis players were not viewed favourably, but there were far worse in the eyes of the Islamists. And I was male, Muslim and a shi'ite.

Let's look at those criteria one by one. Thanks to the revolution, the status of women was completely changed within a few months. Under the Shah everyone lived out his religion in the way he understood it. In our family, for example, my mother had always chosen to wear the veil. My sister, on the other hand, never covered her hair. Until the revolution. From then on, things got corrupted. In the early days of the revolution, a woman who didn't wear the veil risked simply being sneered at. Then sneers became insults; and insults became beatings. Some women were beaten to death, others got acid thrown in their face; others were soaked in petrol and burnt alive. For a woman going around bare-headed, a prison sentence was the result, at best. In practice, they all wore the veil as soon as they stepped outside. But generally they preferred not to go out at all.

Apart from the situation for women it was that of non-Muslims which was synonymous with danger. Until the revolution, Jews and Christians in Iran had complete freedom to practise their religion. The Armenians and orthodox Catholics thrived, whereas in Turkey they had undergone a genocide. I don't mean to say that Iran was a paradise of tolerance, but there was no institutionalised religious discrimination. All that changed with the coming to power of the fundamentalists. Christians and Jews fled, and the Armenians withdrew more into their own community.

The ones who suffered most were the Baha'is. The followers of this religion worshipped a god called Baha'u'llah. There are around fifty million followers worldwide today. Most of them used to be in Iran, but they have been chased out. A friend of mine, an airline pilot who was a Baha'i lost his job soon after the revolution but was able to leave the country before the purges. There were many Baha'is who were simply hanged.

It was the start of a dark period for intellectuals, too. It was they who, at the start, had brought about the departure of the Shah and the fall of his regime. Students and their professors, fed up with the abuses of power by some of the Shah's cronies, had decided to launch a coup d'état. But the intelligentsia didn't have a charismatic leader to take the reins of power. Therefore they associated themselves with the religious movement and in particular with Ayatollah Khomeni who, during his long exile, first in Iraq and then in France, had never stopped opposing the Shah and therefore enjoyed tremendous popularity. The deal at the start was clear: once the coup had been achieved, Khomeni would hand over power to the intelligentsia. Clearly that's not what happened. Installed as head of state, Ayatollah Khomeni scooped in every kind of authority and let none of it go. He consigned one or two ministries to the lay intellectuals at the start of his reign but soon took them back, justifying this action by saying that some of them were plotting coups to overthrow him. Many intellectuals who had been instrumental in creating the revolution ended their lives, hanged like the Baha'is, killed by their former allies....

You will understand that everyone else was subjugated to a feeling of terror at this stage in Iran. Everyone was afraid, because, in the eyes of the mullahs, everyone had something of which to be ashamed.

Receiving the Revolution Cup. I was winner in the singles and doubles of this tournament. My prize was a return ticket to Athens. In the end I chose to go to France.

Chapter Thirteen

THE FINAL NIGHT

I don't know if I was inspired by this non-stop fear, the prevailing uncertainty or the feeling that I would be continuing with this unconventional way of life, but it was at this time – just after the coming to power of the mullahs – that I began to write a private diary. It was a small orange exercise book in which I scribbled frantically, writing down everything that happened to me in a simple, direct style. Without embellishments.... On the opening day of the Revolutionary Cup I wrote the following lines: "I have no confidence in the Council of Guardians of the Revolution. They have agreed that we can organise this tournament, but they will have their pound of flesh in some way or another...."

My doubts about the reliability of the mullahs and my lack of training didn't prevent me from playing well. Or rather, playing better than the others. I won the singles as well as the doubles. Easily. The winner's prize was a return ticket to Europe, or at least that's what we were promised by the clerics in charge. Against all expectations, what they promised came to pass; but the Tehran – Athens ticket which they gave me confirmed my aversion towards them. In my mind, Athens wasn't really Europe. I was hoping for London or Paris, possibly Munich or Geneva, but Athens ....What would I be doing there? When I received my trophy and the air ticket at the ceremony held at the Hyatt Hotel, I didn't think for a second that they were offering me the one-and-only opportunity of leaving Iran and re-launching my life. On the contrary, I was so piqued despite my victory that I offered the ticket to my girlfriend, saying that she could change her mind-set by having a good time in a country where you didn't have to wear the veil.

I was depressed. The standard of my game overall was deteriorating markedly. I was a has-been before I had ever been. The courts of my childhood were sprouting mushrooms, the white lines were peeling off. Bile was eating away at my spirit. I simply didn't believe in my spirit any more. Instead of restoring my faith, this tournament had taken so much organising that I was shattered. My victory allowed me to measure everything I had lost. I was about to founder in depression. Luckily Rima was there.

Rima was a year and a half older than me. I had met her, for the first time, one summer's morning at Amjadieh, just after my twentieth birthday. She was having tennis lessons from a friend of mine. I warned my friend that I was going to nick his client from him ....

Rima was a brunette, very much a brunette, with a serious expression. She had the allure of a soft-skinned, pale-faced queen. I loved being with her. But there was a problem; she was Armenian and an Orthodox Christian. Her parents wouldn't contemplate a Muslim fiancé. They weren't really racists, but the Armenians were a minority and preferred to inter-marry to avoid extinction. So on the few occasions I went to her house, Rima introduced me as her tennis coach, which actually was true.

We laughed at our little secret, but actually it didn't make life any easier. She couldn't come and live with me, nor even to stay the night unless she enlisted the support of a girlfriend to provide her with an alibi. Her mother was no push-over, but we had to be careful. Our relationship couldn't become official. Fortunately, the places where we hung out were not really ones where we risked being seen by her relatives. We went to all the places frequented by young Iranian people. We went to the Chandelier, a restaurant-cum-night club which closed just after the revolution. We also used to hang out at the bar of the Intercontinental Hotel where the prohibitive prices limited the clientele to Iranians with money. She liked to spend the evening in a cabaret club called the Shokoofehno where the best singers in the country were groomed. We were in love, and I had the money to provide a pleasant life for us, which we didn't begrudge ourselves.

Rima worked in an architect's office, spoke fluent English and had very sound taste: indeed she had done the interior design for my house. She could have had a brilliant future outside Iran. But I think she recognised what her future was. She did palm-reading and read tea-leaves. No doubt that's why she often had a melancholy and disillusioned look. She knew that this kind of existence wasn't going to last. In spite of her melancholia she was a terrific support for me. Without her I think I would have submerged completely on that voyage across the waters of the Islamic revolution.

So that evening, after the prize-giving at the Hyatt Hotel, I donated the ticket to her saying: "Go and unwind a bit over there. When you come back you can tell me if you think there's a future for us in Greece. And, if so, we'll try to get there."

At first she agreed, but then, two days later, she had worked out how to convince me with her simple words and practical approach: "Mansour, I've made some enquiries, and if you pay a supplement, you can exchange this ticket for one to France, to Nice, for example. You should go there. There are lots of Iranians already settled there: they can help you to stay, to find a club and to play. Once you're established, I can come out and join you. If you fail, at least you will have tried. You can't stay here and settle for not being a tennis professional. It's what you have always dreamed of, and you should still fight for it...."

Fighting is what I decided to do. You needed determination to leave Iran at that time. You needed two visas, apart from the plane ticket. The first visa was to leave Iran, the other to get into the country to which you were travelling. In most cases Iran refused to issue an exit visa, and for those few cases where you got the authorisation to leave, it was the country of destination which would refuse entry. However, I held a trump card: Reza, one of my best friends, knew the foreign minister in the first Iranian Islamic Republic government, Sadegh Ghotbzadeh.

I didn't realise it then, but I had hit on good timing. Only a few months after my request, Ghotbzadeh was condemned to death and hanged, having been accused of fomenting a coup against the Ayatollah. I'm not sure if it was really what he was intending or if it was the help he gave to would-be exiles that cost him his life, but in any case the fact is that it's thanks to him that I was able to leave Iran.

I had entrusted my passport to Reza, and two days later I got an exit visa, as well as French and Swiss entry visas. I had my ticket amended, and it was now Tehran-Nice, Nice-Geneva and Geneva-Tehran.

Why Geneva? Because I remembered the offer from the manager of the Hotel La Réserve. Why Nice? Because, as my fiancée had said, there were quite a lot of wealthy Iranians who had lived there since the revolution, among whom were my former sponsors who were used to spending their holidays on the Côte d'Azur. I was sure they could help me find work, to get papers and find somewhere to live. I believed they had as much influence in France as in Iran. I didn't think for a moment that they were immigrants, albeit rich ones, or foreigners in France. In my mind powerful people were powerful wherever they happened to be. I was completely wrong. They still had their money, of course, but that's all they had. I wanted to earn my living and expected they would find me a job as easily as someone would point you to the nearest restaurant.

So it was that, on 7th August 1980, a few hours after my great escape from Iran, I had persuaded myself that my former network of benefactors would save my bacon again. But deep down, I felt a horrible sense of doubt growing ….

I remember my last night in Tehran as if it were yesterday. I went to my parents' house where all the family had gathered. They were even sadder to see me go than I was to leave them. I was too preoccupied with the future to grasp that I was abandoning my tribe. I was used to leaving them at the start of my ATP tours, so my departure now didn't seem to take on a different meaning; I was leaving for a longer trip but not once and for all.

We had dinner with hardly anyone speaking. From time to time one of us tried to lighten the atmosphere with a bit of humour, but it all fell flat. My father was staring out into space and didn't speak a word throughout the evening. We spun the meal out and then had tea, all in aid of staying together for a bit longer. When the time came to say goodbye, my father took me in his arms. It was the first time I saw him weep. I felt my strength failing, my heart giving out. Then I understood what I was about to do. But I didn't have any choice now; my mind was made up, and even he couldn't make me change it. The thought did rustle against the back of my mind, but I quickly swept it away. My father was a tough man, and in showing me his tears he gave me the proof of his absolute confidence. If I had let it be known that these tears were weakening my resolve and moving me towards a decision to stay, I would have broken this confidence. No, I didn't have any choice.

With hindsight I know what was making my father cry that night. He was sure that we wouldn't see each other again. Usually, when I was leaving on a trip abroad, he would say: "God be with you, play well!" But this time the emotion had been much too strong for him. He was sure that this au revoir was an adieu in disguise. I started to think that, too, but blocked the idea out of my mind. The thing I am proudest of is that I managed, despite all the hardships I was going to have in France, to see him once more before he died.

My pilot friend suggested meeting up at the airport so I could minimise the searches that could sometimes take hours. The clerics were worried that Iranian people leaving – and who might not come back – would take gold or jewellery with them. They ferreted around and confiscated anything of value. And those who were caught were sentenced to lashes of the whip ....

My friend was late. I waited for him at the entrance to the airport building, appalled. Hundreds of panicky people, men, women, children and old people were queuing in chaotic fashion. Revolutionary guards were abusing them and pushing them around as if they were cattle. Men were sweating, women buckling under the weight of their luggage, with children clinging to them crying and screaming.... It was a nightmare. When my friend arrived he pulled me in his wake and we moved effortlessly through the checkpoints. He took me as far as the boarding gate and, after saying our goodbyes "my" pilot left me to sink into my seat where a stewardess offered me a glass of imitation champagne.

My plane took off around seven o'clock in the morning from Tehran on that 8th August 1980. It was around ten o'clock when I landed at Nice.

Chapter Fourteen

DESTITUTE AGAIN!

On arrival I wavered for about an hour in the arrivals hall at Nice-Côte d'Azur airport. I turned round and round, wandering without knowing where to go. I was terrified at the thought of going out and facing up to my solitude. Nice was supposed to offer me a future, but where should I begin to look for it?

Of course, I was used to foreign towns, aeroplanes, airports and hotels, but so far everything had been planned for me; I knew in which hotel my room had been booked, and I went there with friends, in a group, and with the purpose of competing in a tournament. Now I was left to my own devices, and I didn't know what to do.

After an hour of paralysis I realised that this inertia was shameful. I uttered some insults, aloud, to spur me on and get me out of this torpor into which I was slipping. "Am I stupid or what? I've done the most difficult bit, getting here, getting out of Iran. Now I have to go and find myself somewhere to lay my head." I went to the tourist office. I puffed out my torso and adopted my finest smile. I thought I looked pretty smart in my splendid grey striped suit which had cost a fortune two years earlier when I had bought it during a tournament in Florence (I must have gone once or twice and spent double my earnings in clothes and shoes)…

My seductive Persian attire didn't do me much good. Flabbergasted at my look, the receptionist at the tourist office must have seen a few like me every day. When I asked her, in English, to find me a modestly-priced room for that night she looked me up and down and simply said: "A room? On the 8ᵗʰ August? In Nice? I'm afraid we can't do anything for you."

Crushed, I picked up my suitcase, took my two Yonnex green aluminium rackets and went out on to the Promenade des Anglais. I was knocked out. I walked on slowly without thinking what I was going to do. I didn't notice anything, just kept on walking. I didn't look for a solution. But, as I went alongside the beach, my attention was caught by the bodies of the women and I thought I must be the victim of a hallucination. Scores, hundreds of women, some with their families, others on their own, and some almost naked, in thongs, bikinis, most of them with their breasts on full view!

My eyes were popping out of their sockets. I had to hold myself back from yelling out like the wolf in Tex Avery. Six hours earlier I had been in Tehran where women were no longer allowed to show their hair, where the mullahs required that they cover every inch of their skin and there, on the beach, in full view of everyone, women were going around almost naked with complete ease.

I don't know how long I stayed rooted to the spot watching this spectacle, looking completely transfixed, but the people round me were eyeing me strangely. A swarthy bloke with a big moustache, not speaking a word of French, dressed in a grey woollen suit in the middle of summer on the Promenade des Anglais, ogling the naked ladies on the beach, that could easily frighten the onlookers and attract the attention of the constabulary. Before any of the passers-by could call the cops I started walking again. When I asked someone, in English, where exactly I was, I got no answer at all. People hardly looked at me and didn't even slow down as they heard my "Would you please...." To be frank, the French, on first acquaintance are hardly pleasant or welcoming.

On the beach at Nice, in the summer of 1980, two days after my arrival in France.

I am sitting on the balcony of my house in Tehran, just before my departure for France. I am in the Italian suit I wore on the flight.

It was only hunger and thirst which brought me to a halt; otherwise I would have got to the Italian border without realising it. I bought myself a sandwich and two Cokes. That cost me sixty francs and my final hopes. I only had two thousand dollars in my pocket. I realised that I had no chance of making my nest-egg last until I found some work. While continuing my long march I racked my brains to think through the problem. And there, in front of me, stood the casino ....

With luck, I thought, I could make five or six times the meagre amount in my pocket. In any case, I had nothing much to lose.

In less than an hour I was cleaned out. I managed to keep fifty francs for another sandwich and a Coke. Nothing more. I was touching rock bottom and was almost relieved. This time I had no choice; I would have to go back to Iran on the next flight. It was too bad that I'd be the laughing stock of Tehran for the next few weeks. I set off to look for the office of Iran Air in the town. I walked for another two hours, probably, before I found it. I booked my return for the following day and felt depressed, because this time my failure was going to be obvious. I dreaded having to explain to my father that I had blown all my money in the first casino I had come across. He would never be able to understand why, with two thousand dollars in my pocket, I wouldn't be able to stay long enough to find a club which could take me on as a pro' and a player. Two thousand dollars for him would have been a fortune. With that amount he could live, in his way, for six months. What was I going to tell him? That in France women went around with nothing covering their breasts and that a sandwich cost as much as ten meals in Iran? That's how things were when, coming out of the Iran Air office, I heard a familiar voice saying, disbelievingly: "Mansour, is that you?" I know, it's hard to credit. I ask myself the question sometimes: how is it that, each time I touch rock bottom, a fated jolt from nowhere brings me up to the surface? I don't know ....

I was going to leave France, go back to Tehran and abandon tennis. It was almost done and dusted. I had in my hand my return ticket, my ticket of surrender. And now, behind me there was an old friend who recognised and hailed me.

At the Stockholm Tournament in 1989, with Farokh Moazad with whom I had been reunited by chance in Nice; it was Farokh who had saved me from returning to Iran. We are with Andre Agassi, his brother Philippe and their father who used to box in Iran.

Jahangir Nazemian, my sponsor in Iran. He saved me when I had just lost all my money at the Nice casino.

I had known Farokh Moazed in Tehran when I was sixteen or seventeen. He was fifteen years older and had just got divorced. He had married a very beautiful Swedish woman in the nineteen-sixties and had followed her home. After they split up he wanted to see Iran again, and that's when we met.

He played tennis really well, and as he arrived in Tehran he signed up for a tournament in which all the country's best players (apart from me!) were playing. And he beat them all. The following week, he turned up for another tournament, crowned with the halo of someone who was unbeaten on Iranian soil. But this time I was playing and I beat him hollow. Once his disappointment had eased – it must have been hard to lose against a sixteen-year-old brat when you're already Iran's number one – we got on very well, and he became like a big brother to me. His advice was always sound, and I never doubted his good intentions towards me.

In 1978, because of the tragic events which were starting to unfurl, Farokh left Iran again and headed back to Sweden, his adopted homeland, where he soon found an excellent job. He continued playing tennis and would often appear in tournaments in Sweden and other countries, such as France, for example, where he spent his summer holidays on the Côte d'Azur.

God alone knows why, on the 8th August 1980, his path happened to cross mine. He later told me that, if he hadn't gone to have a nostalgic look at the Iran Air office, he would have passed a few feet away without ever having seen me. In that event, the whole course of my life would have been different.

We talked for about an hour, with me telling him about my journey, how I arrived, the casino and my despair…. He told me the same thing over and over again: "Stay here. You mustn't waste your whole life going back to Iran. We'll find an answer to your problems." But I was deaf to his advice and couldn't see a solution. He persuaded me, nevertheless, to come away with him. He was competing in a small tournament in the hills above Nice and was due to appear in the final against someone called Yves Appelghem who was president of the Tennis Federation of the département of the Var. Farokh was sure he could help me.

Mr Appelghem listened to me and was visibly interested in my story. I told him I was a member of the Iranian national team before the revolution and that I had helped beat the French team in the Galea Cup. He had heard about the rout of the French team. I told him briefly about my best performances on the ATP circuit and, as a closing line, told him he was probably my final hope of remaining a tennis professional. His reply cheered me up for a few minutes. He made me a proposition: "I'll put you in for three or four tournaments in the region. You'll get a French ranking roughly equivalent to what you would have had at the level you were describing to me. After that month of competition, come back to see me, and we'll see how things stand. You have to understand, I'll have to check your actual standard, but if you're the kind of player you say you are, there shouldn't be any difficulty in finding you some work."

His words gave me new hope. For five minutes. Then I realised that, without any money, I couldn't even try my luck. How would I travel to the tournaments? How would I feed myself for a month? And where would I sleep? After all those thoughts I was more depressed than before my talk with Yves Appelghem. But, again, fate brought a stroke of luck.

When I opened up to Farokh with my dark thoughts he smiled and said: "I was holding back the best until the end. You really have got an unrepeatable opportunity. You know who's in Cannes at the moment? Jahangir Nazemian."

Mr Nazemian. The man who had launched me on my career, my first sponsor, my godfather. Indeed, he could get me out of this hole and lend me some money to put me back on the road. But I was ashamed to have to own up to him why I hadn't a penny in my pocket, ashamed to have to ask for his generosity again. Seeing my hang-dog expression, Farokh understood and telephoned my benefactor's hotel.

An hour later we met up with Mr Nazemian in front of the Ritz Carlton. While he was hugging me, he related the story of his life since his departure from Iran. He fled the revolution in 1979 to settle in Paris where he was given residence status; this allowed him to invest in France but not to work there. He had to settle for receiving dividends on his financial assets in France. He was getting really bored and was thinking about leaving France for Canada. He knew he would easily get Canadian nationality and was thinking of going first to New York with his new passport. He already owned some golf clubs and tennis clubs around the Big Apple. Today, he is still in that position ....

We spent only about an hour together because he had an appointment. But those sixty minutes allowed me to bounce back. Thanks to him, I had two thousand francs with which to start my life again. Two thousand francs and three tournaments to find my feet in France.

Chapter Fifteen

DODGY HOTELS

Before playing in the first of my matches I had almost a week to kill and nowhere to sleep. Farokh had been obliged to go back to Sweden two days later but had helped me to ferret out a hotel. We had worked the Iranian grapevine, and he dropped me off very near the hotel Negresco. Unfortunately that wasn't the palace in which I was to reside. Behind the Negresco there's a little street which is dark, even in the middle of the day and where there is a far less luxurious hotel .... I have forgotten the name of the establishment, but I did make a note, in my private diary, of the name of the hotel manager, a fellow-countryman of mine, disagreeable and mistrustful, a Mr Teherani, a name he couldn't have invented .... He looked at me indignantly, doubtless because of my threefold lowly status: newly arrived immigrant (whereas he had been in France ten years); poor (whereas he was a hotel owner, albeit of a shabby one); and, to top it all, an unknown tennis player. I took a room for fifty francs a night.

Luckily, Teherani was never there. He employed, on starvation wages, a young Iranian student who worked twenty-four hour shifts. He was called Hamid, and we quickly struck up a friendship. He always scraped together for me at breakfast-time a few croissants left behind by the other guests. We talked together a lot, and that did me a power of good, to have someone to talk to because, after Farokh had gone, I had started to get depressed.

For the 9ᵗʰ August I noted in my private diary: "Went to walk along the beach with Hamid. He was less surprised than me seeing the bare-breasted women. We talked about that, concluding that Iran hasn't taken the right path with the Islamic revolution. I told Hamid that women caught on the street in Tehran without their chador had acid thrown in their faces. He said he had heard of that."

The first tournament for which I had been entered was in Toulon. Years later someone called Fabrice Santoro came up to tell me that he remembered me; that he had been a ball boy in that tournament and that he had been very impressed by my style of play and my tenacity. It's true that I was playing like a starving desperado. As usual. I lost in the final at Toulon. Out of the three tournaments, I won two and was runner-up in the final of the third.

Mr Appelghem had done me a big favour, first of all by entering me for these tournaments and then by granting me a high ranking. Thanks to that, the tennis promoters were obliged to pay for my lodging. In Toulon I was in a hotel for sailors, probably a knocking-shop, and it was fairly grotty. The next week, in Saint-Raphaël, I slept in a room above the bar in the clubhouse. I shared the room with the barman, who was gay and was forever walking up and down casting lustful looks at me. That didn't stop me winning the tournament, though.

By the end of August I was proud of my tally. I felt that I had still not regained my top form – you can't stop playing for so long without damaging consequences – but my drive to improve had made up for the physical and technical shortcomings. Three tournaments, two trophies and a runners-up medal, it wasn't too bad for an unknown freshly arrived from nowhere. But it didn't earn me the fortune I hoped for. The prize money, for a start, was less than fifteen hundred francs and, even though I was fed and housed during these competitions, I still had quickly to find a job and some reliable income. Unfortunately Yves Appelghem had been rather optimistic during our first discussion. When I went back to see him at the end of the summer, in his office in the hills above Nice, he met me with some sadness. I understood, even before he said to me: "I have heard about your results, and I offer you my congratualtions. You were right, you are a top-level player; but the best I can do for you is to offer you a letter of introduction to Philippe Chartrier, the president of the French Tennis Federation. He may be the only one who can help you. I can't. Your nationality is a real handicap, and the fact that you have just a tourist visa means I can't find work for you. If you follow my advice, you'll go to Paris, get an appointment at his office at Roland-Garros and try to persuade M. Chartrier. He's a good man, and I think he'll do whatever is within his power."

I booked my air ticket and went back to see my friend Hamid to buy him a drink and tell him how I had got on. I wanted to telephone Rima, too, to say that I hoped to find something in Paris. But when I opened the door of the hotel I could see from Hamid's expression that something serious had happened. He blurted out: "War has been declared. The Iraqis are trying to invade. All the flights to Tehran have been cancelled, and the telephone lines have been blocked."

The anxiety caused by those words didn't leave me for months.

Chapter Sixteen

STATELESS AND HOMELESS

9th September 1980. In Paris. I hadn't planned for a single second to visit the Eiffel Tower, the Louvre, the Champs-Elysées or the Sacré-Coeur. For me, in Paris, there was only one attraction: the promised land, Roland-Garros. Having only known clay courts in Iran I headed, on arrival at Orly airport, straight for the Mecca of tennis.

I was apprehensive and excited at the same time. Everything was going to be O.K. because I was a tennis player and I was headed for tennis's heaven. I hadn't any doubt that people would recognise me there as one of theirs. This would be all the more true because I was carrying a letter of recommendation. I was going to find a club that would welcome me, with a job the next day, and I would get my immigration papers within a week.

I handed my letter of recommendation to Régine Tour, secretary to Philippe Chartrier, president of the French Tennis Federation (the FFT). She seemed to be moved when I told her my story, in my still rather faltering English.

She directed me to a small hotel on the Boulevard Exelmans, near Roland-Garros, where I could stay for just thirty francs. That's where I dropped my bags that 9th September 1980. I was worried for Rima, for my family and now for my country at war, but I was also driven by an urge to prevail. I wanted to find myself a place in this new country. That wish has never faded.

Starting the next day I got stuck in to what was to become my daily routine for the next few weeks: going in the morning to the prefecture on the Ile de la Cité to try to extend my visa; waiting in the afternoon outside gate 13 at Roland-Garros for someone to offer me a game ....

After a few days everyone who went often to Roland-Garros knew my story. Those who spoke English had heard it directly, the others had heard translated versions of the strangest anecdotes from the life of this swarthy moustachioed man who waited all day for someone to knock around a ball with him. Some felt concerned and tried to help me; others couldn't have cared less.... the usual story.

I had been advised to see Pierre Barthès who ran a tennis school at Cap d'Agde and was often looking for tennis coaches. They told me he often dropped in at Roland-Garros. I came across him one day and introduced myself nervously, asking if he had any work for me. He listened attentively, but I could see him twitch when I said I was Iranian. He told me he had taken on an Iranian coach a few years before, and that it had ended badly. When he told me the name of my compatriot I understood why it had been a bad experience for him.

Nemat Nematy. A good tennis player, member of the Iranian Davis Cup squad, but a real gambler. He was famous in Tehran for having won more than a hundred and fifty thousand pounds at blackjack one evening before losing the whole lot at roulette the next evening in the same casino. That was at the beginning of the nineteen-seventies. Fairly soon after that he was bogged down in debt. As he owed the casino more than a hundred thousand pounds he fled the country. He left Iran without saying good-bye to anyone, and nobody knew where he was. He had gone to Cap d'Agde and the Pierre Barthès academy. As usual he had borrowed money before gambling it all away and then fleeing for good.

Underneath his sinister shell, he was an amusing and talented character. In Iran he had bought a superb German car, a Ford

Taunus which he had to sell to pay off his debts a few days after he had taken delivery of it. I had an appointment with its new owner at the tennis club. There I was, with my friend Moharam Kodaï, a Davis Cup colleague of mine who had a rather annoying habit: every ten or twenty seconds he would look straight up and make a grimace. The purchaser seemed to have made up his mind, and the deal was about to be struck, but he was still wondering why Nemat wanted to sell this car three days after he had bought it. He thought he could smell a rat, but looking all over and around the car, he couldn't find anything wrong with it, not surprising as there wasn't anything wrong. He was just getting his money out when he saw the expression on Moharam's face. He was grimacing while looking up at the sky. The buyer thought: "He's trying to tell me something." So he kept one eye on the car while glancing from time to time across to Moharam who did his rictus and upward look again. Finally, the buyer said to Nemat: "I don't really like your car. There's something which doesn't seem quite right. I'm not going to buy it." Nemat was deflated and couldn't understand. He went off, furious. At this point, the chap asked Moharam what the hidden problem with the car was, and Moharam answered, logically, with his uncontrollable tic, that there wasn't any and that he had just passed up on a great deal.

I explained to Pierre Barthès, therefore, that not all Iranians were cast in the same mould as Nemat and that I wasn't looking for a hand-out but for work. It was very kind of him to offer me some work after his bad experience with Nemat; but the wages were only enough to feed me, not to provide a roof over my head. I turned him down and waited for a real opportunity to present itself. It never came.

So my sad routine resumed. Each morning I went back to the prefecture to seek an extension of my visa which was due to expire on 29th October. Every day I was refused. Régine Tour helped me with renewing all the administrative procedures to try to remain in France and to try to find a club which might let me join in order to play in team matches. She tried everything, was sincere and a real consolation, but no offers resulted, and I was in a terrible situation: no money, no work, no lodging and, soon, no visa. So I sat outside gate 13, the entrance used by players, and waited for some opportunity to arise. I remember having offered my services, in English (as my French was so poor), as sparring partner to Jean-Claude Massias who was coaching a young hopeful called Guy Forget. Jean-Claude accepted, and we played a match with Guy, who must have been seventeen or eighteen, on court 5. I won, and Guy was furious, breaking some rackets, angry with himself at losing to some unknown Iranian. I was happy, not at having won but at having been given the chance to play. Normally I had only one or two chances a week to knock a ball around; but every day I would spend the afternoon, sitting in the same place, hoping....

One day I saw Nastase practising with Vilas, but I didn't dare go up to introduce myself. I was afraid of disturbing them, and I wasn't sure they would recognise me. When they went to gate 13 to hand back the balls to the person in charge, Ilie recognised me immediately. He was obviously touched to see me again, and Guillermo likewise. They told me that there were people on the circuit who thought I was dead, hanged by the mullahs. They were genuinely pleased to see I was still alive and, I felt, willing to help; but when Ilie asked if he could do anything for me and if I was O.K, I couldn't own up to being in a critical situation. Nothing was going right at all, but I didn't want to burden him with all that, to let him know my real situation. My pride prevented me from speaking the truth, and I said: "Of course I'm O.K., everything is going fine...." When they had gone I dropped off my racket bag in the watchman's hut and left for my night-time tour around Paris....

I had hardly any money left, and I wanted to save the remainder for food. No more money meant no more hotel.... I was of no fixed abode and about to become stateless too. I lived on the streets but didn't want to become a beggar. Despite the direness of my predicament, despite this single baguette which amounted to breakfast, lunch and dinner, despite all these indications of deprivation, I decided that I wouldn't become a tramp by sleeping outdoors on a bench or on the ground. I had no other choice than to stay awake. So I walked all night. Deep down I knew that once I let myself go by sleeping under a bridge or on a bench, I would lose my dignity and never recover it.

So I walked in order not to go under, thinking of what I had to do next day to get a visa, of my daily talk with Régine who would tell me if any clubs had answered the advertisement which she had placed for me in "Tennis de France" : "Ranked player seeks a club for playing in team matches and possibly for coaching." I made endless lists in my head of things I had to do the following day. I would dream while still awake. I fantasised about having a French passport and imagined myself training every day at Roland-Garros with the best French tennis players. I could see myself beating them, hitting passing shots at full stretch, making winning smashes and unbelievable volleys; I re-ran the dreams which had filled my childhood thoughts at Amjadieh. Dreams of glory, of winning titles, of epic contests cheered on by the crowd. I could see myself lifting the trophy at Wimbledon after walking between the traditional lines of ball boys and girls. These pictures consoled me while I waited to raise my head above water again. I kept my head hunched down on my shoulders and pursued my silent, lonely walking.

I paced the streets of the sixteenth arrondissement, going as far as the Champs-Elysées, winding my way along the most beautiful avenue in the world, turning into side streets, then parallel streets until the time came to re-trace my steps. When tiredness became too painful I would strain to keep nothing inside my head, so that I could focus on putting one foot in front of the other. I must have looked like my father when he was teetering home in the evening after his long day of labour. Like him, I felt greatly stressed. But, unlike him, I was alone, without even the joy of having a son walking with me, and that was just as well. Thanks to my solitude I was able to accept my situation relatively philosophically. When despair risked getting me down, I would reassure myself with the thought: "It's not too bad, no-one else has to put up with your hard slog; imagine what it would be like with children, that really would be terrible. You're lucky to be on your own; so stop complaining and remember there are some people in the same position as you with kids to feed...."

That was how I spent my nights in Paris, in October 1980.

The following day I would repeat my supplications to the prefecture, always in vain, before taking up my look-out post again, in front of gate 13 at Roland-Garros.

Chapter Seventeen

WELCOMED

On 26th October 1980, three days before my due date for expulsion, my contact at the prefecture – the only one, in fact, who spoke a little English – made the following suggestion to me: "Either you give us back your Iranian passport and we give you political refugee papers which will allow you to stay in France and travel anywhere in the world or you have to leave French territory before the 29th October. The corollary of having political refugee status is that you won't ever be able to go back to Iran."

It was very tempting. If I didn't have a family still in the country I would have done it without any difficulty and it would have changed my whole life and career. I could have resumed my life as a globe-trotter, competed in tournaments all round the world like any other international player. Who knows what level I would then have reached? I weighed up exactly what my obstinate holding on to my Iranian passport meant. I was probably about to screw up my career, but I couldn't give up the chance of seeing my parents again. They were already quite old, and it would have been very selfish to write them out of my life in that way. When I got a call, three years later, telling me that my father was dying, I jumped on the first plane to Tehran and was at his bedside when he passed away. I would never have been able to forgive myself if I hadn't been able to be there at the end.

On 27th October 1980 I had only two days left in France and

went to compete in my last tournament, at Aulnay-sous-Bois. I was aware that everything was about to finish, but didn't really have any regrets. I had tried everything I could and had failed. There was nothing left now but to go back and try to earn my living in Iran. I couldn't find any other solution. I could still have used my ticket to go to Geneva, but I didn't have the courage to go and start again in a city I hardly knew. I had used all my bravery and energy to make it work in France and had failed. If I look closely and honestly at my state of mind at the time, I have to admit that I was simply relieved. It was over. I was going home.

The Aulnay tournament, would give me the chance, I thought, to turn this final page with at least some style. I was to get lodging throughout the tournament, and at least that was better than walking the streets of Paris.

When I was writing out my request for lodging to the umpire, a chap behind me introduced himself and offered to put me up. Daniel Meyer was a good player and a tennis coach. I accepted his offer and asked if he would be willing to train together before having to play out the final rounds. It was already four days since I had hit a ball, and a good session would do me no harm before starting the competition. He took me to his club, at Villepinte, which is ten kilometres north of Paris. We played, had lunch and met Jacques Raine. Daniel explained my difficulty, and the director said that I could stay and he would try to extend my residence permit. He would sign me up to play for the Villepinte team, and he would allow me to give coaching lessons to whoever wanted to sign up with me! I remember his words: "You're welcome here." You can't imagine how much those words meant to me. "You're welcome here...." It was the first time anyone had spoken to me like that since I had landed in France. Welcomed....

The urgent thing was to regularise my position with the prefecture. Jacques Raine knew a commissioner of police who had the authority to extend my visa temporarily, by a fortnight at a time. Having listened to my story the commissioner, a keen tennis player, agreed to help me, whilst explaining that he couldn't go on extending my visa indefinitely. I would though be all right for two or three months.

Once this was done, I could begin working. Daniel Meyer put me up, and, in return, I agreed to do his tennis coaching when he had other things to do. My first client was called Pierre Degasperi. He looked a bit bewildered when I told him, in my broken French, that I was standing in for Daniel; but I quickly realised that he appreciated my coaching style. I ran after every ball and tried to return them correctly to my client who, for his part, was hitting balls stupidly and generally sending them out of court. I didn't feel at all discouraged as I went to recover the balls and to feed them relentlessly back to him. I told myself that this amounted to training for me and that I should never miss a shot, even if it was from five yards behind the line. Having seen me sweat like a pig for a whole hour, Pierre Degasperi called one of his friends: "The new coach is terrific; you must give him a try." Thus I created a clientele for myself and made some friends.

Daniel put me up for about a month, and then relations with his girlfriend got a bit difficult. She must have been fed up with having me get in the way, and I understood that. I found a room very near the club. I say "a room", but actually it was more like a cellar, located under the bar where I had breakfast (usually a camembert sandwich) every morning. I explained to anyone who was surprised that I could live in such a forbidding place that I had spent my childhood living in similar conditions, except that there were six of us in that place....

I reached the end of 1980 in a state of relative serenity. I had no guarantee how the following year would work out, as I had very little idea of what the future would hold; but at least I had a roof over my head, some friends, some work and, best of all, I could hit a ball around every day.

I was learning French, too, with some eminent professors. My friends Pierre Degasperi, Bernard Fouquet, Günter Nagi, Pierre

Fontaine and Jacques Raine took my education in hand. I made astounding progress. When I asked them how to chat up a lady politely in a disco they told me, with the seriousness of the Pope himself, that I had to say, with a disarming smile: "You are so pretty and look like a gorgeous slapper." After the first slap across the face, I understood. But I had to put my confidence in them and was keen to learn. They told me how to reply to basic questions, then adding that, when introduced to some important man, I had to reply: "Pleased to meet you, you raging pervert." Naturally, I followed their instructions. The worst occasion was when an important commercial lawyer who played tennis at the Villepinte club asked Daniel Meyer and me to a swanky dinner in his flat on the Avenue Foch. There were about a dozen guests, mainly couples, Swedish, American, South African, Swiss and French. The conversations were in English, which helped me. I don't know what got into me when I launched into a complimentary reply in French when the hostess asked what I thought of the meal. I repeated what Degasperi and the others had taught me: "It was disgusting, quite simply disgusting." The instant I finished uttering my "compliment" all the other conversations stopped; even the Swedes had understood.... I blushed, began sweating but was alert enough to explain to my hostess that my French tutors weren't always wholly serious. It got me out of a tight spot but, when I saw them the next day, I was really livid.

I have to admit I didn't stay hopping mad for long; we had a good laugh despite the direness of their japes. I was an extraterrestrial for them, rather in the way I had been for the players on the international circuit when I began in 1976.

I hadn't changed much since that time. I was still hooked on the vice of gambling. Degasperi and the others loved to see me going round the slot machine in the clubhouse bar as soon as I had eighty francs in my pocket after a tennis lesson. I could hardly ever resist it for more than a quarter of an hour before trying my luck and losing the lot practically every time. At least I had the enjoyment of making my friends laugh. I was happy, too, even though my situation wasn't a bed of roses. I felt at home in my tennis shoes, and I contemplated the future without too much anxiety.

1981 began in the same way but, right at the beginning of February, Jacques Raine came up to me one morning with a strained expression. He put it to me point-blank: "I've had the commissioner on the telephone. He can't do anything more for you over your visa. In a week you'll be an alien without official status. I'm not going to throw you out, and you can do coaching for anyone who wants lessons from you. You've got your tennis licence, so you're still a member of the Villepinte tennis club team. But if the cops do a check on your papers they will throw you out, and no-one will be able to do anything for you. I'm sorry, Mansour, you'll have to be careful walking around and about. The main thing now is not to get yourself noticed...."

I can assure you that fear may not last long, but it marks you for life. The fear of the police, the fear of being picked up. The fear from feeling guilty. And I was feeling constantly guilty. In the beginning I felt that everyone was looking at me strangely, that everyone I passed in the street or in other places knew that I had something of which I could be ashamed. The strangers at the bar above my little cellar all became policemen, in my paranoid mind.

Fear soon gives way to a dull anxiety, a diffused uneasiness. Without official papers one is never at ease. You try to reason with yourself, to say that a little tennis player isn't really of any interest to the police and that the police have got better things to do. But you're afraid of a chance happening, a stroke of bad luck. You know that, after the slightest spot of bother, you won't be able to put things back together again. I lived for three months in this way. At the start I didn't take any chances. Then I decided to forget the risks and re-start my life's journey. I played in tournaments and did coaching. And I went back to waiting outside the Roland-Garros courts....

Chapter Eighteen

SAVED BY ROLAND-GARROS

Arriving in Paris, I had been right to think that I would find my salvation there. My intuition hadn't been based on anything concrete, but it had been correct. Three weeks before the start of the French Open, Jacques Dorfman, the tournament referee, gave me a once-in-a-lifetime opportunity by offering me a wild card, which meant taking my chances in the qualifying rounds in the middle of May.

I practised as usual. I was proud that I had been given the chance to compete with the élite of world-class tennis players. After winning two pre-qualifying matches plus my five qualifying matches, I was put into the main draw. In the first round I came up against Jean-Louis Haillet who was ranked number four in France. I wasn't the favourite – far from it – but despite being tired (it was my sixth match, his first), I beat him fairly easily in four sets. My performance attracted the attention of a few journalists who sniffed a good story and weren't disappointed. The first articles appeared the next day. They portrayed an Iranian exile – you didn't find those very often in those days in the sporting world – while the Iran / Iraq war was at its height, with, as a background, the story of the American hostages held in Tehran …. A "good story" for the press. My second-round match would give the journalists the opportunity to get even more out of it.

Mel Purcel was ranked among the world's top twenty tennis

players. He was a very good player, an American, not very cunning but gifted. We were due to play in the late afternoon because there were four other matches scheduled before us. So I was finishing a quiet but copious lunch in the restaurant reserved for players when Chris Lewis, a player from New Zealand came in and said: "Mansour, hurry up! I've just heard the final call for you. If you're not on court in five minutes, you'll be disqualified." At that time there wasn't any TV in the players' restaurant, and one couldn't hear the loud-speakers which gave the results and forthcoming matches. At first I thought it was a wind-up, but seeing how agitated he was, I realised that he was serious. I picked up my sports bag and ran like a demon while my body was struggling to digest the enormous meal I had just eaten.

I arrived in a sweat on the court to hear Mel Purcel asking why I hadn't already been eliminated. I offered my excuses for my late arrival and went to shake Mel's hand. He looked at me with a malignant air, refused my outstretched hand and called me an "Iranian arse-hole." I kept my cool, reassured somewhat by hearing the whistles directed at him by those in the crowd who had heard his remark. The match began, but I could hardly move as I was so full of food. I lost two sets before I could even control my shots. I won the third, but it was already too late. The Purcel machine was rolling, and I couldn't stop it. After he had won with the final stroke he refused again to shake my hand. He left to the sound of booing from the spectators, saying "Get lost!" to the ones within earshot.

The scandal attracted the attention of the press and, as it involved the unknown Iranian who had knocked out Jean-Louis Haillet, a lot of journalists came to interview me. I told them my story, explaining that I was an underground refugee from the régime of the mullahs. My message was repeated many times over on the airwaves, supplemented by commentaries along the lines of "How can France, defender of human rights, turn away Mansour Bahrami when it gave asylum to the Ayatollah Khomeñi a few years ago at Neauphle-le-Château?"

François Mitterand had just been elected president, and France was experiencing a burst of sympathy for human justice. All the papers published my story the day after my defeat at Roland-Garros. Never before had a losing player in the second round of the French Open stimulated such media attention. Following the advice of some friends, I decided to exploit this notoriety which was as new as it would be short-lived by asking for my status to be regularised. Farhad, one of my Iranian friends also in exile in France but living in much better conditions than mine, knew the prefect of the département where I was living. He asked for an interview, and a few days later we went to see him, at the prefecture building in Bobigny, with a bundle of relevant press cuttings.

The interview lasted less than half an hour, and we spoke mainly about tennis. Before my friend and I left, the prefect put in a call to the immigration service, and when I came to the prefecture in Bobigny the next morning my *carte de séjour* was already prepared. It was the same chap who had asked me to choose between being a political refugee and leaving France who handed it to me; he behaved as if he had no recollection of me.

It may seem ridiculous to anyone who has never lived clandestinely, but this piece of paper changed my life. It was my mentality, first of all, which was changed. My spirit was calmed because I was no longer at risk of being thrown out at any moment. Also, even if this *carte de séjour* didn't allow me to travel abroad freely, it did allow me to compete in all the French tournaments. I had become a tennis player almost like all the others, at least on French soil.

For the 8th August 1981, the last page in my private diary, I wrote the following sentence: "I'm going to play, in a moment or two, in a final match to qualify for the main draw in the tournament at Royan. I won yesterday, and I have the feeling I'm going to win again today. It will be a good note on which to end this journal. I think everything is going to turn out all right ...."

I was being a bit too optimistic.

Chapter Nineteen

THE GIRL ON THE CHAMPS-ELYSEES

My sudden fame had provoked a huge demand for my lessons at Villepinte. Everyone wanted me as their coach, and so I began to earn my living properly. With my visa sorted out I had been able to rent a flat three hundred yards from the club. It was a small two-room affair which had belonged to an old lady who had just died. One of the walls was scorched where she had had her cooker. In places the wallpaper was torn, but that didn't bother me much, as I was so glad to have a place of my own. One of my friends had given me a fridge which doubled up as a table. I had a mattress, a table and a dustbin which I could turn upside down to serve as an extra chair if I had a guest for dinner. It was real luxury ....

One fine day I decided to buy myself a cupboard. I had been told about a furniture store five or six kilometres away. I went there and, once I had chosen and paid for the one I wanted, I asked the sales assistant to assemble it for me. Once that was done, I lifted it on to my back and carried it home. The onlookers I passed killed themselves laughing, but I couldn't really understand why. I didn't know anyone with a lorry, and I didn't see how I could have done it differently. My big mistake was to walk in front of the club before I got it home. All the lads were there, and I acquired a veritable escort on the rest of the way home. It was a noisy, jocular escort. What had I unleashed? I hadn't shed the habits of my homeland. In Iran, if you buy a wardrobe, there isn't any delivery service, and you do what you can to get it home. Practically everyone would know someone who had a lorry. This story of the wardrobe would pursue me for years afterwards. So many times, at the club or in the street, people would come up to me and say: "Hey, Bahrami, what have you done with your wardrobe?"

Despite these jibes, my life was beginning to get a bit of order to it. My life was becoming gentle, amusing, almost easy. It wasn't as easy as in that period when I had my own home in Tehran, but almost. I spent all day coaching or playing tennis and the rest of the time having fun with my friends. I was twenty-five, and finally was leading the life appropriate to someone of that age.

Two friends were living in the same building as me. Our favourite game was to wait at an upstairs window with a bucket of water and tip it on to the first one of us to pass below. Our neighbours were perplexed to see us always using an opened umbrella whether going in or out of the building, whatever the weather.

A bit of wealth came my way, and I decided to invest some of it in a car. Up till then it had been Bernard Fouquet who had driven me to tournaments in the area around Paris in his stinking Simca 1000 (we had slipped a slice of Munster cheese into one of the ventilation ducts and, by the time that he found it, there was nothing to be done – the perfume was permanently all-pervasive). I was expecting to be travelling further afield and didn't want to be reliant on anyone, so became the owner of a decrepit old Renault 5. It was Jacques Raine who sold it to me for four thousand francs, payable over four months. Having my own car was the ultimate symbol for me of having settled in France. I was now ready and was going to propose to Rima, as I had promised.

I had been calling her at least twice a week since communications with Iran had been re-established, and we wrote to each other a lot as well. I wasn't being entirely faithful to her, but she was still the one who was in my heart.

On this occasion the conversation was brief. I described

my improved position so that she would understand that I was awaiting her arrival. I would be able to provide the all-important accommodation certificate for France to agree to issue her a visa. I was just about to offer to go and buy an airline ticket for her when she burst into tears. "I can't come, Mansour...." Her sobbing was so strong that she couldn't get the words out. She simply took a deep breath and said: "I'll write to you, and then you'll understand." I couldn't sleep that night.

Her letter arrived. She explained that her parents were opposed to our marrying, that they would not accept her marrying a Muslim and that her mother was threatening to kill herself if she came to live with me in France. She went on to say that she loved me and that I was the only man in her life, that she would never forget me but that we should split up. I called her straightaway, trying to convince her that her parents were bluffing and that eventually they would end up by not holding it against her but that she shouldn't give in. As I was so insistent she started crying again, saying that she would always love me but that nothing had changed. I hung up as I had no further arguments to use. There was nothing more to be said. The second of my serious love affairs had ended.

My friend Morteza, the airline pilot who had helped me to leave Iran, came to see me on 31st December 1981 to celebrate New Year. I drove him in my dilapidated Renault 5 to the Elysée-Matignon, a fashionable disco; but the atmosphere wasn't very good, so we decided to have a look at other places. I tried to go up the Champs-Elysées in the car to find another club. Unsurprisingly, on that day, at that time, all the traffic was jammed. There wasn't going to be much chance of us getting out of the jam within an hour. We were resigning ourselves to spending the first hour of 1982 side-by-side in my moving dustbin when I saw, in the car stopped alongside ours, a magnificent-looking girl. I got Morteza to wind down his window and I launched into English, to avoid uttering the kind of inanity inspired by my friends at Villepinte. I asked her about French customs: was it true that in France people kissed at midnight on 31st December to celebrate New Year? She confirmed that this indeed was the tradition, and so I got out of my car saying: "It's midnight." She seemed to take fright at this and said: "Be careful, there's a dangerous dog on the back-seat." But, finally, she agreed to get out of her car to kiss me. We carried on talking there for at least an hour, in the middle of the Champs-Elysées. Morteza was getting bored to death, but I just couldn't stop talking to her. I thought she was so beautiful I didn't want to leave her. When the traffic jam started to ease she agreed to come back for a drink with us. In the early morning we exchanged telephone numbers, and two days later I was granted a first date.

Frédérique worked as an interpreter and, occasionally, as a reception hostess at international fairs. We stayed an item until the end of that year when I started questioning whether this girl was right for me. She was returning to France from Spain where she had lived until her divorce and she was as adrift as I was. I knew that my parents, especially my mother, wouldn't take kindly to my tying the knot with a divorced woman, so I began to prepare the ground for a separation.

I went to see her at an exhibition centre where she was working. But when I got there, the chap who had hired her said: "You're Monsieur Bahrami? You should please go and see Frédérique. She's gone home sick; she really didn't look at all well…." I got home and found her sleeping, looking stiff and very pale. I woke her up, and she said she felt very ill and wanted an aspirin. She didn't seem to be thinking quite clearly. Still I got her to say that she had already taken six or seven aspirins without feeling any better. I drove her to the hospital at Villepinte where they told me: "It's not serious: it's sure to be a dose of 'flu. Put her to bed, and she'll be in a better state tomorrow." I wasn't at all convinced, and was a bit put out when I called her father and he advised me to take her straightaway to the Ambroise-Paré hospital where he knew the director. Frédérique lost consciousness while we were in the car. I was speaking to her, but she didn't hear anything.

She was almost dead, and I was crying like an imbecile, realising that I was about to lose the woman I loved. The intern who dealt with us soon diagnosed meningitis, and he told me, without mincing his words, that Frédérique had a one-in-ten chance of pulling through. I was shattered and guilty at the thought that I had wanted to leave her. The more I understood the severity of her condition, the more I recognised how precious she was to me and how much I loved her.

Eventually the doctors told me nicely to go away, telling me they had done all they could to save her. They said we now simply had to wait either for the illness to subside or for Frédérique to pass away.

The next day she regained consciousness, but the doctors were still reluctant to give a prognosis. I spent the whole day at her bedside holding her hand. I was saying over and over again: "You've got to live. For me. Don't leave me alone." She said, feebly: "But why are you saying that when you want to leave me? I don't want to live any more...." I was terribly emotional. I was so moved I didn't know what to say to her apart from repeating that I wanted to stay with her; I promised that I wouldn't leave her. When I tell my friends the story I usually finish by saying: "Tough luck, she recovered and I had to keep my promise." The truth is that I was the happiest of men on the day when the doctors told me that she was going to pull through. But she still wasn't back to full health. I had to feed her with a spoon for more than six weeks after her release from hospital. She could hardly move. Then our life together resumed; and a year later we were married.

During this time the situation in Iran was becoming really serious. The war with Iraq was causing thousands of fatalities, and even though poverty wasn't affecting my family in Tehran too much at that time, I knew that they risked suffering in the days to come.

I was telephoning my mother twice a week. Even at the most critical times in my life, I never let slip this reassuring routine. My mother couldn't have borne not to hear my voice, so when I didn't have enough money to pay for the call I resorted to System D. In the days of coin-operated phones there were several methods of making cost-free calls anywhere in the world. Like all the immigrants in France, I knew the designated phone booths where you could talk for hours on end with someone in France or abroad with a single coin jammed into the box. This racket was a practical one, but it had two major disadvantages: first, you had to queue for ages because I wasn't the only one who knew about the defective booth; secondly, the France Télécom engineers would eventually spot the problem and come and fix the phone in the booth, thus making me go out and look for another. One day, while queuing with half a dozen foreigners by a "free" telephone booth, an old African awaiting his turn gave me a gold tube.

One needed a bit of dexterity to apply his method, and it didn't work every time, but I became an expert. The trick was to slip a coin into the apparatus while pressing gently on the black button which triggered a refund of your money. Once the coin started to be accepted by the phone, you released the black button as smartly as you could. If your timing was good the coin stayed jammed, and I could talk to Iran for as long as I wanted. On those occasions I prayed that no-one would come and settle in next to the booth. I was scared of my name being given to France Télécom or even to the police – especially during that period when my residence status was dodgy – and I was so ashamed to be hogging the telephone while others were waiting that I often gave in and hung up before really finishing my conversation.

It was through such trickery that I learned my younger brother Iradj had decided to enlist in the mullahs' army in order to fight the Iraqis in the south of the country.

It was my mother who told me about it. I could feel, after a few moments, from the tone of her voice, that something was not quite right. She passed the phone over to my brother. I tried to reason with him, saying it was irresponsible to go to the front when he already had five children, that no-one would be there to look after them if he got himself shot. I told him that his war should consist of making sure his family were properly looked after and that was less visionary but just as noble a mission as the one he was planning. I offered him my concept of real heroes, those who were unseen but performed their duty making those around them happy. But his mind was made up, and he told me again that the Iraqis had invaded our territory and were raping and pillaging. It was a waste of time arguing with him; he was consumed by fanaticism. We agreed to stop discussing it. He left for the front line at the end of 1982.

At the house of my brother Shirzad (on the left) in Tehran in 2001, with my other brother Iradj.

He was there for eight months and came back a changed man. His rhetoric had been tamed, and on the rare occasions when he agreed to talk about his war, I realised that he had gone through a traumatic experience. On the telephone he told me that he was just as patriotic as ever but that he had seen Iraqis falling as they were shot. I suppose one doesn't kill one's fellow man with complete impunity. He told me of the nights in the trenches when lack of sleep brought hallucinations. He told me of his fear and of corrosive ever-near death, of the heroism and baseness of men going out to die and being blown up by mines. He had enlisted in a brigade which had liberated Khoramshar, a town in the south of Iran. He described for me the ruins, the inhabitants trapped in their houses for months before they could tell their saviours of the pillaging and raping perpetrated by the Iraqis.

The time he spent on the front was a long period of anguish for my parents and for me. My mother passed on the rare snatches of news that she had received. Iradj called when he could, which was two or three times a month. He wrote more often, but that didn't prevent my parents being worried sick. As usual my father didn't let his feelings come to the surface, and when I was speaking to him, he didn't touch on the subject, preferring to ask about my game, the matches I had played and my life in France. Naturally, as I had done since the beginning of my exile, I jollied up my adventures, more to stop him worrying than to put myself in a good light.

Thanks to my father's meagre pension, they got by without too much difficulty. My mother went to see her children and grandchildren quite often; my father seemed at last to have found some peace, albeit in a resigned sort of fashion. He told me he spent his time with his friends, at the mosque, and that his life was good, the only thing missing was the pleasure of seeing me. He and my mother really wanted to see me again, without ever owning up to the dread of not seeing me again in their lifetimes. I felt that too, and conspired in not bringing the subject out into the open. Deep down I had promised myself not to let that happen to them. This thought burrowed into my spirit: I wanted to see them again, once more, before they went.

And what was happening on the tennis front all this time? Well, I can admit now that I made the most of what was on offer. It was practically impossible to leave French soil, so I trawled across tournaments the length and breadth of the country, notably in the Marlboro Tournament which was positioned in ranking, at that time, just below the ATP tour. I criss-crossed the mainland of France in my old white Renault 5, Frédérique at my side, to compete in the score of contests staged each year.

I was winning some important trophies, and each victory brought points. We were fed and housed, and whoever had amassed the most points at the end of the year earned a bonus worth around fifteen thousand pounds. That was a decent sum at the time, and there were quite a lot of us competing for it. There were quite a few foreigners, including several Argentinians specialised in clay court play, plus often players returning from the ATP circuit and those between major tournaments trying to scrape together some more winnings. Such was the pool in which I was competing. It provided the opportunity of pitting myself against the top level players, and I wasn't often beaten ....

I started competing on the Marlboro circuit in 1982. First I pulled off the doubles title, partnered by Bruno Dadillon. We didn't lose a single match! By the end, when our opponents saw that they had been drawn against us, they wouldn't even show up, preferring to offer us a drink to being hammered. On those occasions, in lieu of playing the match I practised or played at backgammon with my colleagues, usually with Loïc Courteau, Amélie Mauresmo's trainer. Once I had such rotten luck playing against him that in my rage I tore up the leather travelling case for his backgammon set. Since then, each time he sees me and he senses I am a bit stressed, he goads me: "Ah, Mansour, let's tear up one or two backgammon sets!"

I had a very good season in 1982. I earned the equivalent of twenty thousand pounds on the Marlboro circuit alone and reached my top ranking in France, in the top fifteen. At the same time I was playing team matches for the Villepinte club, which was rather tame by comparison.

The team used to compete in the regional championship, and I often had to play opponents who only just had a ranking. Often they came up and asked for my autograph before the match! I would sign with good grace and tried to spin the game out as long as possible. Once the match was finished they were focussing on getting themselves photographed with me, which I found quite touching.

I had played against the Moroccan Omar Laimina in 1975 in Tehran. I had beaten him in the first round of the King's Cup, in three sets, but fairly convincingly. At match point, while I was leading 5-1 and 40–15, I won a superb drop-shot but, as I followed through, the racket slipped out of my hand. That didn't give the umpire pause for thought who declared "Game, set and match." Laimina went apoplectic, shouting at the umpire that the point I had won at match point wasn't valid because I had let go of my racket before it had hit the ball which is, indeed, against the rules. In this case, however, it wasn't so, as I still had the racket in my hand at the time of impact. Despite that I suggested to Laimina that we replay the point. He refused, saying that the point was his, and there was no case for playing it again. That wound me up so much that I said: "I'll give you the point." However, the umpire, knowing my volley was perfectly O.K., turned that down and declared me the winner. Omar made such a fuss that he copped a thousand dollar fine, a substantial amount at the time. The worst thing was that he refused to shake my hand as we left the court. If he was obliged to apologise, he did it to the tournament director, not to me.

Ten years later I came across Omar Laimina on the Marlboro circuit. He still had the same surly temperament. As I soon became the number one on the tour and he my understudy there were a few sparks between us. Our matches were always tense, intense and hotly contested. One day I competed against him on the courts at the Aix-en-Provence country club. The umpire wasn't having a good day and made all kinds of errors. At first these were in my favour. But when one of my opponent's balls was called out and I knew it to have been good, I had the point played again. That happened at least six times in this first phase of the match, and each time I passed two balls through to Omar who never thanked me. I had been expecting to be thanked. At the beginning of the second set, when I was leading by quite a margin, having won the first set, the umpire called one of my shots out, when it was well inside the line. I interjected: "No, umpire, it was good, please ask Omar." However, Omar looked at me and said: "No, I play according to what the umpire says. If he says it was out, then out it was." That sent me into a fury. I called him a bastard and reminded him that I had given him the benefit of the doubt five or six times in the first set. He annoyed me further by saying that that was my problem and that "you shouldn't make gifts of points to the other player" in a match. O.K., I won that match and swore to myself that I would never lose against Omar. On occasions that was difficult. He was very tall and served and volleyed: also, he had such good coverage of the court that it was difficult to stretch him with

passing shots. But I held on, at the expense of flying into a rage ....
Sometimes we would end at 14 - 12 in the third set, and sometimes
we came to blows; but I never lost against him. I stayed number one
on the Marlboro circuit, and he number two.

Although these wins in a second league tournament allowed me
to live comfortably, I felt frustrated at not being able to break into
the top level. The problem was always the same; I was practically
unable to leave French territory. Between 1981 and 1986 I must
have competed in only four competitions abroad. Even then, I had
to apply for visas months in advance, with an authorisation from the
prefecture to leave, as well as from the other country to enter. So
I had to settle for ATP tournaments in France – Metz, Bordeaux,
Toulouse, Nice, Monte-Carlo and Roland-Garros – to try to gauge
my level on the world stage. I had to go through the qualification
tournament each time, to reach the final draw. I got there nearly
every time, but that made the competition into a real marathon.
So it was that, in 1984, for the Moselle Open, in Metz, I had to
play and win seven matches to pass through the pre-qualification
and qualification stages to reach the first rung of the final ladder.
I went on to win my initial main draw match, then in the second
round and the one after that. I got as far as the semi-finals, and at
that stage the ATP representative came to see me to say I would
have a dispensation in the next tournament where I would have a
place in the final rounds without the need to play qualifiers. This was
excellent news as I wouldn't reach the final rounds exhausted just
when I had to play the strongest players. The next tournament was
to be Brussels and it carried a purse of six hundred thousand dollars;
it was a major tournament, to be contested by all the world's best
players. I was really excited and asked the ATP guys to help me get
a visa. I said to myself that, even for an Iranian, it shouldn't be too
complicated to get from Paris to Brussels. I was wrong. The chap at
the consulate, when we went to see him, said that it would need two
months, in view of my Iranian passport, before we would have an
answer from the Belgian side and that it would probably be negative,
even then. It made no difference trying to explain to him that I was a
tennis player and that I had been invited to play in a tournament in
Brussels in two days' time: he just didn't want to know. I had to turn
the invitation down. Same every time.

Nevertheless I managed to pull myself up to being the number eight player in France by competing in just the six major tournaments taking place within France, the Marlboro circuit and some rare events (four in five years) in Germany where it was a little easier for an Iranian to get an entry visa than for other countries.

The other players were always telling me that these visa problems were spoiling an otherwise promising career. On the few occasions when I was able to perform in an unconstrained way in this period I got some splendid results, notably in doubles matches. In 1984 I managed to leave France for a tournament in Florence where my partner and I won against Cash and Alexander, one of the best pairings in the world.

During a tournament in Guadeloupe in 1986. I was taking part with Loïc Courteau, Arnaud Boetsch, Jean-Marc Piacentile, François Cervelle and Thierry Pham. I am with Frédérique, my wife, and I am holding our son Sam.

Chapter Twenty

GROWING UP

The Villepinte Club was like a family to me. In 1983, when we had our wedding, it was at the club that we held the ceremony.

17th December 1983. My wedding at Villepinte. My pupils formed the guard of honour with their rackets.

The managers, the people whom I coached and the other players were my best supporters. People often asked me why I stayed at Villepinte rather than join a trendier club. Each time I would reply that I felt at home there. And that was true. However, my assertions were clearly not enough, because Jacques Raine, the president, had many people asking him why I didn't leave. For some time the rumour persisted that Jacques told people I didn't leave because no-one had offered me better terms than Villepinte. I didn't know about the gossip; but one day I overheard a conversation between Jacques and a member of the club. I heard him explain that I owed an enormous debt to him, that it was thanks to him that I had been able to rent a flat, which he had furnished and for which he paid the rent. He finished by saying that if I stayed at Villepinte, where the next best player after me was ranked like an average club player, it was because I hadn't received a better offer.... I chose to make myself known at this point. Jacques blushed, and there was an awkward silence which I broke by saying: "Jacques, I think you were in the middle of a conversation about me. You should know that I have stayed here up till now solely out of friendship and loyalty. It wouldn't have been difficult for me to find better conditions elsewhere because clearly I don't have anything special here. I can assure you now that I will let it be known that I am looking for a new club, and we'll see if I get any offers – or not."

Less than a week later, at the very beginning of February 1984, Robert de Flandres, team captain of the Val de Marne club, at Perreux, offered me seventy thousand francs a year to play in his squad. I came back and told Jacques Raine of the offer I had just received and told him: "I don't want to leave here; if you give me half of what de Flandres is offering, I'll stay." He consulted his father-in-law who was the owner of the club and came back with a negative answer. I was saddened and a bit taken aback. I knew that his father-in-law liked me a lot, and I didn't understand his refusal. It took me some time to realise that he was pushing me to the exit so that I could move up to the next level and climb further.

We left on good terms with Jacques Raine and the others. I

bought a flat in Colombes, signed up with the Val-de-Marne club and began to train every day at Roland-Garros.

I made progress at a cracking pace. After several years of living with a dearth of quality players, I was hitting with Noah, Forget, Leconte, Raoux, Delaitre and the other French stars. I began to achieve correspondingly better performances in tournaments, and certainly began to be noticed for my wins as well as for my unconventional playing style. I was a fierce player but also in love with what for me was the beautiful game. The extraordinary shots I make nowadays on the senior tour or in exhibition matches I was then beginning to use experimentally in "real" tournaments. When replying to a lob I would return the ball through my legs, with my back to the net. I used backhand drop-shots to good effect in base-line exchanges, and I had no compunction, either, about throwing myself to the floor to reach an otherwise impossible ball.

I'm not sure exactly at what point Erik Bergelin, the son of Lennart Bergelin, Björn Borg's coach, noticed me in 1984. He was working for IMG, an American firm of athletes' agents, and also organised exhibitions, notably for Ilie Nastase. Ilie was due to play Tarik Benhabilès in Rouen in an exhibition match: and when Tarik cried off, Eric Bergelin thought of me. I accepted and asked for five thousand francs, thinking: "This is a bit much, asking for five thousand for a match with nothing at stake. He will laugh like a drain!" I knew from his smile, however, that he would have accepted double that ....

The match went very well. The spectators were delighted, and the reviews in the local press the next day were full of praise. Leaving the court Nastase was heard to say: "I've played someone who's even crazier than me." It's true that I had fired off an incredible array of shots. I had served with six balls in my hand, attempted impossible shots and been an out-and-out clown. The spectators were kept happy all the way through, a tangible sign of success. Soon after that Ilie and I received scores of propositions from all round France to play this kind of match. We played between twenty-five and thirty exhibition matches per year between 1984 and 2000 when Ilie stopped playing for good in order to try to be elected Mayor of Bucharest.

This didn't stop me trying to shine on the ATP circuit, especially in 1986 when I was granted a carte de séjour valid for ten years, which made it a lot easier to obtain visas for playing abroad. The consular offices started to conceive it was possible that I was a respectable Iranian person who wouldn't put down roots in a new country, abandoning my wife and child in France. For I had, indeed, become a father.

With my wife Frédérique, at an evening event in 2002.

Chapter Twenty-One

THE REFORMED GAMBLER

I think I have only ever had one vice. But it was a big one, gambling. I was a serious gambler, of the kind who risked one day losing everything in the casino. I had to wait until the spring of 1984 to understand finally that I had to control my passion. It's thanks indirectly to Frédérique that I managed it.

I had just been knocked out in the first round of the Nice tournament. I went to the casino the day before I went back to Paris, and I lost, in the matter of a few hours, around six thousand francs which was much more money than I had earned from competing in the tournament. I left the casino disgusted with myself and, on the way back to the hotel, passed in front of a jeweller's. I looked at the superb jewellery in the window and cursed myself for not having spent the money on a gift for my wife rather than one for the owners of the casino. All the same, I went in to the shop and bought a beautiful watch. Once I got home I handed the gift to Frédérique and told her of my latest misadventure, promising that I wouldn't ever gamble again. I have kept my promise.

That's perhaps what convinced Frédérique to go ahead and have children. She was confident that I would look after her and them and become a suitable father. Well, almost.

I missed the birth of my son and will regret that for the rest of my days. Sam was born on the 4th April 1985, during the Monte-

Carlo tournament. I, like an idiot, hadn't booked in advance a return ticket to go there and back in a day and thereby be able to hear my son's first cry. I stayed at the club, telephoning the clinic every ten minutes. I was so stressed out that, once Sam was born, I said to Mats Wilander who was alongside me: "It's a boy. He's fifty-one metres long and weighs forty-one kilos." Mats, ever the sober Nordic type, came up with a typical response: "That's a fine baby.... I hope your wife didn't suffer too much?"

I didn't commit the same offence five years later when Antoine was born. I was there! It has to be said I hardly deserved it, as he chose to see the light of day during the Paris-Bercy tournament. Guy Forget's wife was also nine months pregnant at the start of the tournament, and she had the same doctor as Frédérique. On the morning of 31st October Frédérique felt the first contractions, and I drove her to the hospital. I was helping her out of the car when Guy and Isabelle Forget arrived. My son Antoine was born at 4 p.m.: Mathieu, Guy's son, four hours later. As Guy and I were each as jittery as the other in those four hours, we went time after time to check on the other one's wife. I went to chat to Isabelle, and he to Frédérique. The nurses weren't sure any more which father was which. For the next week there was a string of players going in and out, as they were all there for the tournament. The girls' rooms were overflowing with flowers, and the procession of people in sports kit was never-ending. The clinic staff couldn't get over it: one moment they were chatting to Yannick Noah, ten minutes later with Boris Becker, then Mats Wilander, Henri Leconte, Stefan Edberg ....

I binge on tennis. I always have done. So when my ten-year carte de séjour came through I started travelling on the ATP circuit and registering for as many tournaments as possible. I had to pass through qualifying rounds because of my middling status. But I did have one distinction of which I'm proud. I was the only player who received guaranteed payments for competing in qualifiers! The organisers of less important tournaments offered the best players guaranteed payments, regardless of the results, to attract them. This unofficial custom only involved players whose fame attracted spectators. Many of the organisers felt that I belonged to that group and offered me handsome sums without being sure I would get through to the final draw.

31st October 1989. The date of the birth of my son Antoine, and of Mathieu Forget. Same day, same hospital.

Around this time I was looking for a partner with whom I could play doubles. For me, it wasn't just about earning more money. It was really about wanting to maximise the number of matches I played.

At the 1985 Stuttgart tournament I proposed to the Uruguayan player Diego Perez that he sign up with me as a doubles player. He agreed, and we reached the final after beating four excellent pairings. As an experiment it had been pretty successful, and we continued along the same track. I don't know how many finals we competed in together. Diego wasn't a doubles specialist, and some players asked me why we were playing together. But he was an excellent base-line grafter and was great at returning the ball. His serve was passable, and we complemented each other well. I liked him very much. He's a bit crazy but is often very funny. So I continued as his partner, and the results flowed in.

In 1986 we went in for the Paris-Bercy tournament, one of the most important tournaments in the world, after the four grand slam ones.

I was with Diego in the office of the umpire Jacques Dorfman when the draw was made. I read the names of our opponents, spitting out at each stage a comment: "First round: Sanchez-Casal [they were the two and three in the world!] – we'll get through that easily. Then Hlassec – Slozil, we should be able to nail them within an hour. After that, it gets a bit hairy: Noah and Forget in the semi-final – we'll have to get ourselves into gear, eh, Diego? We should be able to get through in three sets. After that, we've got a real match on – the final with McEnroe and Fleming, that'll be tough, but we'll have a good time whatever happens...."

The folks in the office were doubled up laughing and said to me: "You're a real big-head, Bahrami. You'll get knocked out in the first round ...." What happened? It went exactly as I had predicted. We got to the semi-final without any problem, then we beat Noah and Forget in three hard-fought sets. On the day of the final the Bercy stadium was full, which is very rare for a doubles final. There was a feverish atmosphere in the stands, which was normal as McEnroe was playing, and people weren't able to see him playing in France very often. We were well on the way: at 4 – 3 against us in the second set I served two aces against McEnroe and was getting ready to serve for the third time against him. I made as if to try for a third ace with a forceful serve but, just as I struck the ball I made my usual gasp and stepped aside, deliberately, to let the ball fall. Then I converted it into a little drop-shot. The ball fell dead, just beyond the net, bouncing once, then twice, then three times. John didn't make the slightest movement. The spectators' mirth increased in proportion to their noticing how sore McEnroe was at being fooled by my bluff. He went purple, and everyone sensed the rage bubbling up inside him. It was grotesque. He shouted at me: "You really are an ass-hole. Who do you think you are? You think that's funny?" I replied: "Yes, it was quite funny. And by the way, the spectators seemed to find it funny, too." He went off and sat on his chair, deflated. Two games later, they won the match, as expected. When he shook my hand at the net he treated me to a cannibalistic smile. It was just as well he won that encounter, Johnny Mac. Otherwise he would have thought I had made him look ridiculous, and I would have become his enemy.

Bercy, 1986. My first important finals match. With Diego Perez. We were playing the pair of McEnroe and Fleming. It was a great moment, despite losing.

Despite his excellent results I had a genuine concern about Diego. In every match, when I was at the net, he would – at least once - serve the ball either into my back or into the back of my neck, sometimes straight into the back of my head. The worst thing was that, every time, he burst into laughter. It's very painful to take a hit from a tennis ball at a hundred and ten miles an hour, and I just gritted my teeth.

In the spring of 1988, during a tournament at Key Biscayne, a major tournament played on an island near Miami, we were up against a player of whom I had never seen even a picture, Brad Gilbert, who was partnering Kevin Curren; and Diego made one gaffe too many.

We had won the first set and won a service break in the second. We were leading the game 30 – 40 on Curren's serve. Kevin had missed his first serve, I was the returner, and I said to Diego: "You go up to the net, I'm going to try a power return." The snag was that powerful returns had never been my forte, and Kevin, instead of doing a normal second serve, unleashed an almighty powerful one. I couldn't respond properly, sending a gentle return towards the other side of the net. Brad Gilbert exploited the opportunity to enjoy himself. He could have placed his shot wherever he liked but chose to volley it with all his might at Diego's head. Before I could ask him if he was O.K., he began to bad-mouth me: "You're a nobody! You'll never learn how to return a serve properly! Thanks to you I've been pelted by a shot from this idiot Gilbert. It's unbelievable, you're really crap!" It was so over the top that I wondered if he was joking, but he really was serious. I asked him to forgive me and advised him to "stay focussed so we can win this match", a match in which we were on top, despite this incident. But Diego started to sulk and to wobble. He stopped talking to me and also stopped trying. Everyone could see that he was playing in a random way. I tried to reason with him, saying that it was a very important tournament, that we had no right to let slip away a match where we were clearly on top. But Diego dug his heels in, and we lost in three sets. Once we were back in the dressing-room, I reminded him of all the balls he had propelled into my back or into my head. I had never made the slightest reproach about that. He, on the other hand, at my first blunder, had behaved like a spoilt child. I wanted us to remain friends, but I said that we couldn't play doubles together any more. It was a pity because we made a good partnership, but I never went back on my decision.

I paired up with quite a few players before finally settling in with Eric Winogradsky who was to become one of my best friends. I'm also the godfather of his son Hugo. It was with Eric, in 1989, that we achieved the best result of our careers.

My friend and doubles partner Eric Winogradsky. His son Hugo is my godson.

Chapter Twenty-Two

IN THE FINALS AT ROLAND-GARROS!

In 1989, at the age of thirty-three, I reached my peak. So many things happened to me that I hardly know where to begin. I do, really, though – with tennis, as always….

Eric and I became a formidable combination on the ATP tour. My notoriety was extending beyond my circle of friends and of those who knew me by enjoying my preposterous tricks. I realised this in Toulouse, just before a doubles match with Eric. We were due to come up against the pairing of McEnroe and Nargiso in the semi-finals. Playing against Mac is really something special: he's a genius at the game. I felt honoured to be on the other side of the net again to such a big beast.

In the tunnel leading from the dressing-room to the court, while we were walking side by side towards the light and could already hear the mounting clamour of the crowd incited by the commentary over the loudspeakers, John McEnroe came up to me and said: "Mansour, please don't try one of your contorted shots. It works nearly every time, and I get the feeling I look really stupid. Frankly, it's not good for my reputation in front of this crowd. Be a nice fellow, try it on my partner if you want, but not on me."

He was genuine and nice about it. I felt incredibly proud. In front of us, the umpire, Gilbert Ysern, who had heard every bit of the conversation, didn't make any objection either. Mac is so proud that it must have taken a real effort to speak to me in that way. I was touched by it and replied: "Don't worry, John, I will be careful."

We played very seriously and won fairly easily. I felt on top of the world because the great John McEnroe had paid me a compliment. God knows he didn't dole compliments out too much during his career.

When the draw for the doubles competition in the 1989 French Open at Roland-Garros was made, neither Eric nor I thought for a moment that we were only a fortnight away from the best result of our careers. Like all the other players we were there to get through as many rounds as possible. But it's a long way from that thought to imagining we would get to the final....

I had dreamt of it for so long.... Even at the age of six, playing with my broom-handle, in front of the wall. Twenty years later, walking the streets of Paris to avoid having to sleep on a bench, I had also thought of this glorious day, the day I would play in a final at Roland-Garros.

It had been a strange journey from start to finish. That day it was a fine morning, my favourite kind of spring day, with the sun in a softly bright sky. I turned on the radio to hear my name, as if to get independent confirmation I really would be playing in the final, but it was about the Ayatollah that they were talking.

He had died. That struck me as strange. I arrived at the ground at the end of the morning. Some journalists were waiting for me but, as before, they didn't want to ask about the final in which I was due to play. They all wanted a reaction to the death of the Ayatollah, from the lips of the chap who had fled the régime, who had lived in France without proper papers before taking his revenge on his destiny. I understand clearly the agenda they had mapped out: I would be playing the most important match of my life on the day the man who had thrown me out had died. I could see well enough where they were coming from, and above all where they wanted to take the story; but I had no wish to grant them what they wanted. I had no comment to make on the death of Khomeini because I was willing only to talk about tennis. Everything else but tennis was like foreign territory for me. After all, I was in the final in the French Open! And our opponents were to be Jim Grabb from the USA and Johnny Mac's brother, Patrick.

I was focussing on my match. I was working it out: we would go on court after the women's final which brought the German Steffi Graf up against the Spanish Arantxa Sanchez. I thought we would probably start our match around 4.30 p.m.

It didn't happen the way I expected. First, the clouds began to build up over Paris, and a thin, icy rain started to fall. I don't remember how many times the women's singles final was interrupted. Eric and I, in the dressing-room, were playing and re-playing the match in our minds. We were fast losing the adrenalin we were going to need.

The Graf/ Sanchez match was going on for ever. It was probably a magnificent match, but I didn't see any of it. All I remember is that I found it too long! Arantxa ended by winning in three sets, with the last one finishing 8 – 6. Eric and I walked on court at 7.30 p.m. to play our final. It soon became really cold and, to top everything, the French rugby final was due to begin at 8.00 p.m. The upshot was that about fifty people were in the stands, and I knew half of them by their first names ....

That sapped my energy. This wasn't how I had envisaged playing in the final at the French Open. I wanted to hear the shouts of the crowd, feel their warmth and enthusiasm. I wanted to light up the spectators and the court. But how could I light up fifty frozen mates of mine who had come along simply to be nice to me? What a nightmare ....

I've never liked going on court when there aren't many spectators; so for the climax of my career it was simply unbearable. I wanted to live out my greatest dream, and it was all going wrong. I couldn't produce quality tennis. My arm felt useless, and I simply wanted to get it over with and leave this place which had spoilt my boyhood dream. I let the match slip away.... I was suffering a kind of torture and knew that Eric and I didn't stand a chance. The score against us was 6-4, 2-6, 6-4, 7-6.

My older son Sam was four. He was in the stands with Frédérique in the section reserved for players and their families. When the prize-giving ceremony began, Sam came on to the court. He probably wanted to come to console me. Philippe Chartrier, the president of the French Federation, who was getting ready to present us with our losers' medals, didn't recognise him and pushed him gently away. Sam didn't like that at all and bit his hand. Today, it makes me smile to think back to that episode, but at the time it was a bit mortifying. Either way, the tactic worked: I took him up in my arms and for a few minutes forgot that I had lost the "match of my life."

At the French Open final in 1989. With my four-year-old son Sam, after the prize-giving.

With the passing of time, the memory of that defeat has softened, and I retain a little happiness at the thought of having reached the final of a grand slam tournament. But it's a scar, too; and when I'm asked – as I often am – whether that was the finest day of my career, I have to say that unfortunately it's more complex than that. It's both the finest day and the most terrible nightmare. To play in a final and lose amounts to a trauma which cannot be erased. Except by winning another. But I haven't had that chance. At least not in a grand slam final.

With my sons Sam and Antoine, in Florida, in 2000.

Chapter Twenty-Three

MY DUSKY FACE

The first grand slam of the season is in Melbourne in Australia. I went there once, in 1975, before the Iranian revolution. The Australian Open is the grand slam tournament where an outsider has the best chance of making a mark, perhaps even of pulling off a coup. There's quite a culture of doubles playing in Australia, and I really wanted to compete on a court where the stands are filled with an appreciative crowd. But I needed an Australian visa.

At the Australian consulate in Paris an official told me I needed to hold a return air ticket for my application to be considered. It cost me, at the time, seventeen thousand francs. Later they told me it would be a long time before I got an answer. I went two months before the tournament and filled in the forms, gave her the letter of recommendation written by the tournament director, and so on.

When I asked, a few days before my departure date, what had happened to my visa, they told me it would be another five or six weeks before I would be told whether I would have it or not! I was wasting my time explaining that the tournament was to begin six days from then; nothing made any impact on them. I collected my passport, threw my return ticket in the bin and went home.

My ten year residence permit issued in 1986 allowed me to leave France if I travelled in Europe; but beyond the continent it got complicated. For every trip I needed the equivalent of two visas again, one for the country where I was heading, the other to be allowed to return home to France. It's hardly compatible with the peripatetic life of the professional tennis player. Also, there are the little pieces of red tape which look harmless enough at first sight but can become, longer term, very constraining for those who are subject to them. As I crossed the border point, going in or out, it evolved invariably in this kind of way: the immigration officer would hardly look at the passports of the people in front of me, simply waving them through. Then my turn came. The official would seem to wake up, look at my documents with close attention, then look into my face with a disapproving look saying, when the theatrical sighs of the person behind me were becoming more oppressive: "Please stand aside, sir, and we'll check your identity...."

Anyone who hasn't experienced this has no idea of how exasperating it can be, when the stares of other people have bored into your back and you don't feel comfortable in your own skin, even when you've done nothing wrong. I had Iranian identity papers at the time when terrorism had become a serious problem in Europe. I had the terrorists' trademark handlebar moustache: so I was automatically a suspect. Each time I disembarked and approached the immigration desk I felt my hands getting moist, my heart beating a little faster. It was simply added stress, the stress of knowing that, a few minutes later, the chap behind me in the queue was going to be skewering me with his stare because he thought I was wasting his time.

All that was taking its toll; and I realised that obtaining Franco-Iranian nationality would allow me to avoid all these unpleasant scenes. I was, after all, married, with two children, and earning more than an average wage, thus making my fair share of tax contributions to the French exchequer. I had been resident for eight years, and nothing should have stood in the way of France adopting me as one of its own.

The procedures took almost a year. I had several interviews with various people from the immigration service and, in October 1989, was summoned for the final round. A nice lady greeted me and assured me outright that I would be able to have French nationality. She explained that this was to be the final stage in the (long) process to receive French nationality and that I now had the opportunity to "frenchify" my name a little. I understood exactly what she meant but played the simpleton. She was a bit peeved, replying that I might want to call myself "Pierre or Paul, or Jean-Jacques, or well, there are many others...."

I put on my broadest smile and asked her: "Do you really think that, with a face like mine, I would be taken seriously if I claimed to be someone called Jean-Jacques?" She laughed and admitted: "No, perhaps it wouldn't really be believable." So, Mansour Bahrami I remained, even if I am Mansour Bahrami, citizen of France!

A week later I received my new passport which I used for the first time for an exhibition match in Germany. On the way there, there was no problem; and I was proud to have this little document in my pocket. I felt that a new kind of life was starting, a life without red tape. I was liberated, just as if, with a bit of paper, I had become a Frenchman like all the others.

On the way back I was rejoicing in the thought that I would pass through immigration like all the people in front, and I was smiling at everyone. The passengers were, as usual, filing past the immigration officer who was hardly looking at them. I arrived opposite her and presented my brand new passport. "Would you step aside, please, Mr Bahrami, we will check your identity." It made me smile. I explained I had only just taken delivery of my passport and that, if I had known that it wasn't going to change the way I was regarded every time I crossed the frontier, I would have stayed simply as an Iranian. That made her laugh but didn't sway her from taking a good ten minutes to study my passport before finally she said: "But Mr Bahrami, you shouldn't have changed just your passport, because now you have a face that doesn't match it." And she gave me a big smile as she beckoned me to go through.

A month later one of my brothers came from Tehran to spend

Christmas at our place. One morning I asked him along to the Australian consulate where I was applying for a visa to play in the Australian Open the following January. I reassured him it wouldn't take more than an hour now that I had a French passport. I had telephoned the consulate the day before and been told that, with my French passport and two photos, I should get the visa in less than half an hour. I had filled in all the forms and we sat down for the expected half-hour wait. People were coming and going, putting in their applications and leaving with their visas while we were still waiting. We had been sitting there for a good two hours before a consulate official asked me, in a rather surly manner: "Mr Bahrami, it seems you applied for a visa in 1986 but under a different nationality. Is that right?" "Yes, that's right, but since then I have been granted French nationality, and I have been assured I would get my visa in less than half an hour." She was still as serious as a judge when she explained that there hadn't been a decision on my 1986 application and that I couldn't therefore make another application until there was a decision on the first one. I was absolutely flabbergasted. Stunned and amazed, I asked her if she understood how absurd it was. I tried to humour her, saying that I was a tennis player invited to play in the Australian Open, but she remained stony-faced. I was furious. I picked up my documents and left. The next day, John Fitzgerald, the Australian champion, happened to phone me, and I related the story to him. He was concerned. He suggested intervening at the Ministry of Foreign Affairs, but I refused his offer. I decided that I would never set foot in Australia, and that was too bad for the first grand slam of the season.

After thirty-three years, in 2009, I did in fact relent and accepted an invitation to go to the Australian Open. The highlight of my trip was attending a luncheon to mark the fortieth anniversary of Rod Laver's four grand slam wins in 1969, quite a year. The four players who were runners-up to Laver were also guests of honour: Andres Gimeno, Tony Roche, Ken Rosewall and John Newcombe. At the luncheon, I was on a table with Martina Navratalova, Jim Courier and Henri Leconte and felt truly humbled, and thrilled, to have been included in this landmark occasion.

Chapter Twenty-Four

NOAH-BAHRAMI

It's usually at this stage in the story of my life that people ask me the question. If I had had my French passport earlier what would have been the difference in my professional tennis career? What level could I have reached? I have asked myself the same question many times, without ever finding an answer. With a passport I would indeed have been able to travel like the other players, progressed more, certainly, and cleared the hurdles that took years to jump by spending years settling for life on the Marlboro circuit. If I had been able to mix with the best players more often, I would have become a more competitive player. I might have ended up by hiring a coach instead of being completely self-taught. That way I might have reached the top 50 in singles and the top 10 in doubles, or perhaps even better in the world hierarchy. Perhaps.... Would that have changed my life? Certainly. Would it have been better? Who knows? I am happy as I am, and that's the most important thing. Even if I had been able to carry out my profession more easily, I would have suffered from a serious handicap, from a defect which is probably more crippling at the top level: I like the beautiful game too much!

The passion for tennis has always consumed me, and it has often overwhelmed the competitor within me. On many occasions I have sacrificed winning for the sake of a fine piece of theatre to entertain the crowd or to make sure a match lasted longer. How many times have I yielded points to an adversary, when I am in command, simply to allow him to get back in the saddle, give him a bit of hope and stop him throwing away the match? This approach is probably not consistent with being at the very top of the sport. Of course, I have snatched victories by digging in to avoid defeat, leaving my entrails on the court from seeking a win at all costs; but I haven't done that systematically, and at the highest level you need to be able to do it at every opportunity.

I don't put a match to bed in the way that Jimmy Connors, for example, knew how to do so well. The English expression "the killer instinct" expresses it best. Jimmy Connors took it to extraordinary lengths. It was as if he often wanted actually to "kill" his opponent. It was visible when he went to the net and hit the ball as if he wanted to make it explode, as if he was plunging a knife in. I have never wanted to be like that throughout a match. I have never known how to cut a rally short, how to concentrate on my opponent's weak points.... Also, my best memories in tennis are not all of my victories. I have been quite happy to leave the court acclaimed by an appreciative crowd who have been cheered up and kept amused for an hour or so. It's true that, as soon as I realised my strengths as a player, I have always played for the crowd and not for the win. I know that I am far from having reached the top level in the game, but I know, too, that the best players enjoy playing with me. What's even better is that they enjoy watching me play. That, for me, is the best form of appreciation.

The match I played against Yannick is, in a way, the match that changed the course of my career. But I lost it. As so often it was from wanting to play too much. But on the day after that match, in November 1987, people recognised me on the street and asked for my autograph. I lost, but after that match my work colleagues, stars of the game or simply unknown players would often come to watch me play, thinking that "something is going to happen" and that, in the worst case, they will at least "have a good time"- or that's what they seem to think. The match was held at Bercy....

I wanted to play this match against Yannick Noah, as if I knew in advance that it would change my life. I was already very fond of

Yannick, as a man and a player; and I would have been very excited in any case at the prospect of playing against him, but on that occasion the anticipation was accompanied by a premonition.

To reach this second round of one of the world's major tournaments I had, of course, to get through the first round and therefore to defeat Tarik Benhabilès, the newly-arrived prodigy of French tennis, who was ranked number twenty-one in the world at that time. Not a walkover, then. But I had always performed well against him. From about ten encounters I must have won around seven or eight. This time I won again, in two sets. Tarik was furious. He said I was "unplayable." It's true that I had played really well: I was on top form physically, and my shots had never been so penetrating.

On the day before the big match I heard Yannick talking about me on the TV. He was generous and complimentary, saying I was "a very nice guy who's difficult to play and especially to beat, a guy you need to take seriously because, under his cloak as an entertainer" I was, in Yannick's words "an excellent tennis player, peerless technically and a battler who knows how to go the full distance." I remember he added: "yeah, Bahrami, he's an adorable character, so adorable I haven't won against him yet!" It's true, we had played each other, in doubles matches, three times; and I had been on the winning side each time. In the dressing-room, just before we were called on to court, Yannick was very nervous.

He was focussing. He was going to dig deep and give it his all to beat me. I felt good and knew we were going to play a great match. My intuition was confirmed as soon as we got on to the court. The Bercy arena was full to bursting. The crowd was already warmed up. I don't know if it was the media which had led to this atmosphere, but I felt clearly that something was in the air. It was an expectation, a tension, for the pleasure that was to come. Soon it was to become crazy.

We began tightly, exchanging blow for blow, attempting – and often pulling off – incredible shots, volleys out of this world. After three or four games we were covered in sweat. The radiant faces of the people in the crowd showed their excitement as much as their pleasure at being there. I can't play a match without looking often at the crowd. It's not that I need it to feel whether they are enjoying it or not (I can tell that instinctively): it's that I like to see the faces of the fans in the stands to have a better rapport with them, to let them know that they, too, are part of the spectacle. On that day, looking at the crowd at Bercy, I was surprised to find that there were fellow players as excited as the ordinary spectators. There were more and more people in the stands after every game, aware that something special was happening.

Neither Yannick nor I were fading. There was between us that total confrontation which only respect for one's opponent brings about. We weren't yet the close friends we have since become – and our friendship doubtless owes something of its strength to this match – but we had a mutual appreciation, as people and as sportsmen. That was why neither of us gave ground, out of respect. Respect for the opponent, the game and the public. I derived untold pleasure from playing this match, to such an extent that, sub-consciously, I felt it might never end. That's how I lost it, 6 – 7, 5 – 7. It was because I got wound up and tried an impossible shot at deuce. Because I wanted to give still more to the public. Because, sometimes, I don't know how to stop myself.

After the last point I fell into Yannick's arms. The spectators were on their feet, entranced. The ovation we received was one of the greatest I have ever received. It touched me to the bottom of my heart. After enjoying the cheers for several minutes I went back to the dressing-room. A cluster of players was waiting there for me, together with a few well-known promoters and tournament organisers who were talking to Yannick. They congratulated me warmly, and several of them talked about organising exhibition matches with Yannick. I didn't pay much attention to it at the time, but Yannick had understood immediately. Since then we have played scores, perhaps hundreds, of exhibition matches. The Bahrami-Noah dual has become one of the most popular in the world of tennis.

"Mansour's Seniors' Party" at the Villa Barclay, in Paris, in 2001. Yannick Noah, Arnaud Clément, Sébastien Grosjean, Nicolas Escudé and Bruce Meritt.

At the Paris Country Club in 2001. Yannick kisses my feet as congratulation for an unbelievable shot during a seniors' tournament.

There have been other frenzied encounters since that glorious defeat against Noah in the second round at Bercy. But none has ever reached the sporting intensity of that match. The theatrical, sometimes comic, thread woven through my game started at that iconic encounter, and as it has been developed, my showman's nature has taken the edge off my competitiveness. I think I took this decisive turn towards showmanship in Basle, in 1990.

Tennis fans will remember Marc Rosset. He was a Swiss player, very tall, lanky, and blessed with a monster serve, a very gifted player. He was a stylish chap who, in the eyes of many a talented player, let himself be taken over sometimes by existential doubts which probably impeded his career from being more successful than it turned out to be. But Marc was regularly one of the ten best players in the world. Thus, when I came up against him in the first round of the Basle tournament, he was in the top ten. I was the underdog, even more so as he was playing in front of his home crowd. I rated him highly and wanted to make sure we offered a good show to his fans. Alas, as sometimes happened to him around that time, he was having an off day. I, on the other hand, had a good feel for the ball and was beginning to stack up some winning points, then some games. He was sinking, bit by bit, into a depression. I could see from his expression that he wanted to be anywhere except there, battling to win a game of tennis. But I wanted to play and give the public its money's worth with a bit of pulsation in the match. It's not easy to raise the spirits of the crowd when you're the only one who wants to win the match. I won the first set 6 – 1, and the nine thousand spectators looked on, concerned, as Marc was throwing away the match from the start of the second set. I couldn't stand that, so I, too, began throwing it away, offering him points by making beginner's mistakes. The crowd wavered between booing and laughter, such was our travesty of a performance. Régis Brunet, Marc's agent, was looking at me with a mocking expression from the edge of the court. So I warned him: "He wants to get himself shuffled out of here as quickly as he can, your little foal. He's got no escape because I want to play tennis. And for as long as he won't knuckle down, I'm going to spin out the match!" I continued letting Marc back into the match.

Predictably he took advantage of that to bring the score to one set all. From then on, he started playing his best tennis. The standard of play shot up, as did the atmosphere and the crowd's enthusiasm. I have to admit that, by the end, it was so close that I thought: "What a clot I am! By now I could have been back in my hotel room, through to the next round, whilst now I risk getting knocked out because I wanted to play too much ...." These regrets didn't last too long, as I took the match, snatched in the tie-break in the third set. The crowd was on its feet, and Marc thanked me for having drawn him out into playing properly. The problem was that it had taken its toll on my body. The next day I had to pay for that error.

I was up against my favourite opponent: Yannick Noah. Since our contest at Bercy our matches couldn't be played along conventional lines. That's the cost of success. To add a little of the Harlem Globetrotters to our show, Yann and I went on court dressed up as one another: he sported a superb pastiche moustache; and I was crowned with a Rasta wig. We warmed up with these disguises still on, and the crowd was won over. The problem then became how to measure up in sporting terms after this piece of sartorial clowning and protect our status as professional sportsmen. It was a major tournament.

We began the match at a cracking pace. But I hadn't entirely recovered from the exertions of the previous day. I took a service game off Yann to lead in the first set but, as I was straining upwards for a volley to smash home a point, I felt a dagger plunge into my thigh. All athletes know the pain caused by a torn muscle. They all know that it's best to stop immediately, to get the muscle seen to, so that the damage doesn't go even deeper. I doubted that I would be able to take at least a full month's rest. If I carried on with the match the meter would still be ticking, and I risked not being able to get back on to a tennis court for even longer. On the other hand, I didn't want to abandon the match – something I had never done – out of respect for the public and the organisers. Yannick, who could see that I was in trouble, urged me to stop. The physiotherapist brought on by the umpire advised me also to count myself out, but I couldn't bring myself to do it. So I made a pact with Yann: "You will win the match anyway," I suggested, "and we'll go on with the show." We shook hands on it, and this became the first example of circus-tennis! We brought out all the shots we had tried in training to amuse our friends. The people in the stands were doubled up laughing, and I could see all my tennis-playing friends come out on to the benches. The word went round the locker-rooms: "Get out into the stands, chaps, Bahrami and Noah are letting themselves go, no holds barred...." I saw Connors, Ivanisevic, Korda and many others getting worked up because of what Yannick and I were doing. Sergio Palmieri , Yann's and John McEnroe's agent, was there, too, having a whale of a time. Only the umpire was having trouble following what was happening, not knowing what kind of stance to take. At the end we earned a standing ovation and, since then, I have been invited every year to Basle to play an exhibition match. That's been going on now for almost twenty years ....

Chapter Twenty-Five

BORG, CONNORS AND MCENROE

After this match in Basle proposals for exhibition matches came in thick and fast, and I had neatly slipped away from the ATP circuit to give priority to these show matches which were less demanding physically, more lucrative and above all more in keeping with my concept of the game, based more on spectacle and enjoyment, less on winning. Soon afterwards, I was invited to appear also on the veterans' circuit organised by the ATP. At first I appeared alongside fabulous veterans such as Roy Emerson, Ken Rosewall and Tony Roche, legends from the early days of professional tennis. They had each lifted a grand slam trophy, but that didn't stop them accepting me, with my meagre awards, as one of theirs. We all had fun together, and they seemed to re-discover their youth by coming back on to the court. They had all gone well past their fiftieth birthdays but acted as if they were still at college, singing bawdy songs and chatting up the waitresses in the restaurants, like spotty youths; It was great fun. But it didn't pull in the crowds ....

Then Jimmy Connors took over the reins, and everything changed.

As I alluded to earlier, Jimmy Connors is a venerated big beast in the world of tennis. He has won eight grand slam titles and was number one for years on end. He holds numerous records, including the number of tournaments won (a hundred and nine). He is among the five greatest players of all time. In 1991 he reached the semi-finals of the U.S. Open at the age of almost forty-one! After that he didn't take long to bow out but, as he wanted to carry on playing, he put together a fully-fledged veterans' tour in the U.S. It was an immediate success.

Jimmy Connors and me with the future world number one, Roger Federer, then 13. Roger sent me the photo. He remembered that we had played together in Basle in 1993. My thanks to this terrific champion!

Jimmy had a whole lot of enemies in his playing days, and they would be ready to trot out any number of reasons why he was a despicable fellow. McEnroe, for one, just couldn't stand him. He couldn't find words sharp enough to speak about Jimmy, citing his lack of generosity, his all-consuming appetite for winning and the sometimes inglorious means he selected for getting there. For his part, Jimmy said that Mac was a sick personality and that he belonged in a mental asylum, not on a tennis court; I suppose their sporting rivalry at the time exacerbated their mutual loathing.

Nowadays, they do however manage to share a TV studio

seemingly affectionately and, without question, very effectively. I think both men have mellowed over the years and, based on mutual respect and a healthy regard for the past, have developed a maturer relationship.

I have never had anything to complain about with Jimmy Connors, quite the contrary. As soon as he had launched his tour he invited me to play, as he was hand-picking his players. He wanted only the crème de la crème, the best-known players, all aged of course over thirty-five, those with the most titles and the most spectacular players; there was Borg, McEnroe, Connors, Vilas, Noah and Nastase: and
Bahrami ....

Of the whole crew, it was to Ilie Nastase that I felt closest. First of all, because I had been a ball boy for him when he was playing in the Davis Cup against Iran in Tehran. Also, I had bonded with him quickest when I was starting out on the major circuit, in the mid-seventies, when he was the big star. Our friendship owes nothing to chance. A story had to develop between this over-gifted Romanian, an exile in France, like me, and the accident-prone Iranian Bahrami. Ilie simply recognised in me certain things which he appreciated and understood. I think he regards me rather like a younger brother.

Nastase is a truly exceptional character. He is mad, and a genius. He channelled his creativity into comic turns; I have never known anyone so good at teasing. He gave nick-names to everyone, without caring, sometimes, if he used some exultant cruelty. Thus, I remember the Austrian player whom Nasti called "Monday, Monday" like the famous song of the nineteen-sixties. This chap wasn't a very strong player and so generally lost on the first day of tournaments which were almost invariably on a Monday.

I have seen Nastase eating dinner in striped pyjamas in three star restaurants, in the luxury hotels where he stayed. I have seen him charm his way past the housekeeper after an hour of chatting her up, to get into the room of the Argentinian Jose-Luis Clerc, just to empty an aerosol of shaving foam into his bed. On the same tour he hung on the door of Nikki Pilic's room, a notoriously skin-flint Yugoslav player, a massive breakfast order, fit to feed an emperor, with caviar and champagne, all to be delivered at five o'clock in the morning. This poor chap had to get out of bed at dawn to explain to the waiter that he hadn't ordered a hundred grams of Beluga caviar, nor a magnum of Kristal for his breakfast.

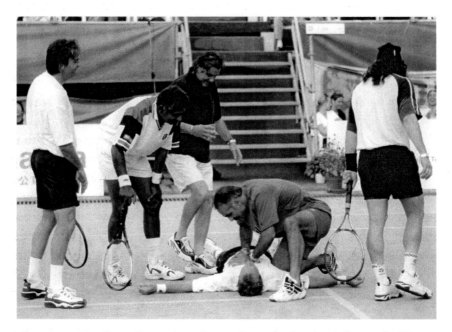

Singapore, where I was watching the match which brought Vijay Amritraj and Henri Leconte up against Vilas and McNamara. Peter McNamara was ill. I came down, out of the stands, with Ilie Nastase, and we set about reviving him. Heart massage was followed by mouth-to-mouth resuscitation.

There's another side of Ilie which I can't leave unmentioned. He will probably call me a liar, but I should then point out that he's the greatest trickster I have ever come across. On the tennis court he would take on umpires but didn't try very hard to cheat: with all other games, however, the cheating is second nature to him. He cheats at backgammon, at golf, at anything where there's a clear winner and loser. We played a round of golf with Manuel Orantes. I couldn't understand why Orantes was laughing his head off. Eventually he said: "Nasti isn't too good at golf but he's a real champion at football." For over an hour Ilie had been giving his ball a nudge with his foot to get another ten or twenty yards with each shot!

That's Nastase in a nutshell. The picture wouldn't be complete if I didn't add that Nasti, before he met his wife Amalia, was the greatest pick-up merchant I have ever seen. Seducing women was his favourite pastime, and I have to admit that he rarely failed.

Björn Borg, also, was a compulsive womaniser before he met Patricia, his mate for life. But, unlike with Nastase, it wasn't the process of seduction which interested him most. Borg is an athlete in the way few others in the world are. He took on sex as if it were a sport, high performance stuff, taking on numerous partners without ever flagging, and with a capacity for athletic exploits. In sport he was only up against men, but off the court he cultivated his appetite for women. He adored them. It reached such a point that, at one time, it was best not to have a room next to his in a hotel, unless you were equipped with sleeping pills and earplugs .... On occasion he would stay in his suite for days on end, as spruced-up top models went in, then came out a few hours later, exhausted. He sometimes didn't put in an appearance in public, to the eternal despair of tournament organisers who had brought him in at great expense and who were wondering if he would be in a fit state to play tennis after his indoor marathons. But Björn has always been a real pro.

His marriage put him on an even keel, his life got taken in hand, and I'm sure that nowadays he's living a more peaceable existence. Björn is someone I have always enjoyed being with; he's so nice, kind and biddable. He's a simple chap at heart who, privately, has not much in common with the public idol he used to be. He certainly suffered from this mis-match between his personality and his public image; but he finally reconciled them. He's happy and deserves it. He is humble and generous. When he takes a taxi, he often leaves as a tip more than the cost of the journey. When a fan asks him for an autograph, a photo or a few words, he always obliges as far as he can, whatever the circumstances. I've even seen a fan wake him up during a transatlantic flight to ask for an autograph, and Björn signed for him, with a smile. I can imagine that if the same fan had tried the same ploy with John McEnroe ....

With Borg on the way to an exhibition match in Tehran. Björn always responds positively to my calls. He's an exceptional champion, and a fabulous and humble man.

There's something you need to understand about McEnroe: he has never faked being angry. He can lose his temper for a trifle. Sometimes it then gets out of hand. He's still a genius, but one who hasn't lived with his gift in the same way as Nastase or Borg. Nasti channelled everything into levity, irony and humour. Borg showed unfortunately, as he approached his forties, some self-destructive tendencies. Mac is also prone to destructive impulses, but they are directed towards others.

On court Mac is allergic to umpires but also is quick to lay into his opponent with insults for reasons which often defy understanding.

Usually the opponents choose to let him get on with it and ignore him. The only one I have ever seen react is Henri Leconte. Nothing surprising there, really, I fear my excellent friend Henri is even more of a crackpot than McEnroe.

They were playing one another in Chicago, in mid-summer, in torrid, stifling heat, laced with humidity. John was taking all the time in the world between points, but when Henri asked a ball boy to fetch him a towel to dry himself down a bit, Mac lost his rag and demanded that the umpire penalise Henri who, as is his wont, was stalling a bit too much. Leconte didn't wait for a second; he leapt over the net and pressed his nose up against Mac's, inviting him to "shut your big mouth." Mac was stupefied. He stood there, without moving a muscle. I was in the stands and thought that he was going to choke with rage. No-one had ever dared to speak to him in this way. Henri enjoyed his little joke, blissfully unaware that he was within a cat's whisker of having a punch in the face from John McEnroe.

Towards me, on the other hand, John has always behaved well - with one exception. I was competing against him in the first round of the Masters in Naples, Florida. I was fortunate enough to be able to win a point against his service and, to put a little more pressure on him and to amuse the crowd, I moved forward a yard or two for the next return. At first he looked at me askance as if to say: "Enough of your antics, Bahrami". But, seeing that I wasn't budging and that the crowd were laughing, he showed some signs of irritation. After a minute of bouncing the ball on the floor and shaking his head, while the mirth in the stands was still rising, he prepared his serve and launched a massive stroke. I tried one of my favourite strokes: the drop-shot with back-spin. The ball shot off spinning towards his end of the court and, on the rebound, came back over the net without John having made a single movement. The crowd stood up, applauding me to the rafters. As for McEnroe, he stared at me, hands on his hips, hate shining from his eyes. He said: "You fucking ass-hole, don't so this shite to me, keep it for the other assholes!" Everyone heard, and it ignited a round of whistling. That made him even madder. "Are you happy now, Bahrami? All these morons are going to hate me now." The onlookers didn't take kindly to this insult and booed him until the end of the match. It didn't upset him any further: he won the match, which was all he was interested in.

Off court McEnroe doesn't worry too much, either, about being boorish and bad-tempered. We were due to be in Geneva for two days to compete in some exhibition matches sponsored by a banker. We were having dinner with Tatum, his wife at the time, in the best Chinese restaurant in town. The players were due to meet up with some sponsors and VIPs at the dinner table. So I wasn't surprised when two couples – the men in dinner jackets, the women in evening attire – came smiling up to our table. They were probably expecting Mac to smile back and to motion them to have a seat; but he ignored them completely. After a minute of excruciating awkwardness for everyone except John, one of them said, in perfect English: "Dear Mr McEnroe, permit me to introduce my wife, my colleague and his wife." John looked at him as if he were looking over a heap of dung on a silk carpet and said: "So, what is it that you want?" Taken aback, the man said that, as principal sponsor of the tournament, he had been invited to have dinner with us. This chap had spent a hundred and fifty thousand dollars of which two-thirds had gone straight into John's pocket who, without blinking, said: "Out of the question. I'm with my wife and some friends, and I'm reckoning on spending the evening with them, and only them." I tried to reason with him, but he wouldn't change his mind, saying that he was "fed up with answering the same idiot questions" which "these shit-faces are bound to ask if I let them sit with us." He finished his tirade with a sentence that required no response: "they can go and fuck themselves!" It goes without saying that our outraged sponsors left; and, the next year, the Geneva tournament had got new sponsors.

That's the caricature of John, a mixture of ex-City of New York and Irish background, but one has to give him credit: he is the player who fills the arenas in which we are playing. He remains the star of the Seniors' Tour; he is the most professional of all of us, and he makes it a paying proposition for the organisers who have to guarantee him a hundred thousand dollars before he will go anywhere. John is expensive, but his participation guarantees the success of a tournament. And I find that he gives value for his money. He earns it even with admirable sincerity, because he devotes to tennis a respect for which no-one could reproach him. He works hard all year to stay fit, he still plays incredibly well and without giving anything away to his opponents. If you haven't trained hard enough he will crush you pitilessly. He won't willingly let you take a point, and at the end of the match, if he likes you and has enough respect for you, he'll invite you to New York to spend a few weeks of intensive training with him. If he doesn't rate you, on the other hand, he will look at you in a disdainful way before tossing out some heartfelt thought about your lack of professionalism.

Fortunately for me, I am lucky enough to enjoy his respect and friendship.

When John set out on the Seniors' Tour, he arrived with his hands in his pockets at the training camp, having understood that he would no longer be able to lift a trophy at a grand slam like the "young ones". He thus took two punches on the chin, and clearly that annoyed him. So he disappeared for several weeks during which time he worked as if he were preparing a great comeback at Wimbledon. When he came back on the Seniors' Tour everyone understood that he was the boss. He played a match against a former world number one and crushed him 6 – 0, 6 – 0. So we all went back into intensive training. Mac pulled our standards up. We didn't have any choice: if we had let ourselves go, we would have been out.

His attitude, although it's humiliating for some of his victims, has meant that the Seniors' Tour has never sunk into pathos. We guarantee everyone a spectacle (the show is more important than the result – and, in any case, the result is frequently the same, McEnroe often wins!), but it's still a sport, and so we owe it to ourselves always to be on top form physically.

After thirty years in the tennis world I have finally made many true friends. I believe I am easy-going, good at bonding and don't hold grudges. I have sometimes got angry with certain work colleagues, but there are very few towards whom I feel hate. Guillermo Vilas, for example, has managed to get me hopping mad. But I finally achieved a reconciliation with him, and today I have a sincere appreciation of him. At the time, however, he succeeded in making me fly off the handle. Quite an achievement.

Guillermo is one of the sacred beasts of tennis, in the same kind of frame as Nastase, Connors, Borg or McEnroe. The problem with him is that he has never accepted growing older gracefully and not being the greatest player in the world. For all the time I've known him, I have nearly always seen him with girls twenty or thirty years younger than him. That's his way of staying young. Once, at an airport, I heard a lad say nicely to him: "Mr Vilas, you were my father's hero. I know you were a very great player." He got as mad as hell and said drily: "I'm still a great player. I'm not dead, you little shit." And he was depressed for the next three days.

Another anecdote comes to mind. We were competing in a tournament in Calcutta, in India. As we arrived at the hotel, a porter rushed towards him, saying: "It's an honour to welcome you to our modest establishment. I am one of your greatest fans." Guillermo puffed out his chest and was starting to prepare a worthy speech in reply – he loved speaking, conjuring up elaborate sentences, reflecting his second calling as a poet – when the porter stole his thunder by adding: "Indeed, it's a great honour to welcome you among us, Mr Borg." Guillermo turned green, and I thought he was going to cry. As for me, I couldn't help bursting into laughter. But I soon stopped when I saw Guillermo was genuinely wounded. He is sensitive, Guillermo, even emotional on occasions. But his anguish sometimes lets him down.

We were in an important tournament in Columbus, Ohio. For the first time in my career, I had asked a friend, Arnaud Casagrande, former coach of Escudé, to come and give me some coaching. All the usual crowd were there: Noah, McEnroe, Borg and the others. I was to play both singles and doubles, like Vilas, and the luck of the draw brought us up against each other in the first rounds of both singles and doubles. In the doubles I was partnered by Vitas Gerulaitis, whilst Guillermo was playing with John Lloyd. Vitas and I won quite easily, but Guillermo refused to shake my hand at the end of the match, which I couldn't understand. Once we were back in the locker-room I asked why. There, in front of my friend Arnaud, he said: "You haven't learnt from history, Bahrami. You're a stooge in this drama: you play and amuse the public; but against me, Connors or McEnroe, you're supposed to lose. People don't buy tickets to come and see you. They come to see stars like me, and you need to behave so that I'm not knocked out when I play you." I didn't say anything. Guillermo Vilas had been one of my heroes when I was a boy: I had a photo of him, when I was about fourteen or fifteen, doing a smash, and he took my breath away now, telling me that I should throw a match away so that he should win ..... Despite the surprise and disappointment I managed to tell him that I found his words perverse and that he would understand his mistake when we played singles. The next day we played at full stretch. And I beat him.

In the locker-room again, neither he nor I dared look each other in the eye. Eventually I made the first move. I said I had always held him in such high regard that he had been for me one of the world's greatest players, but if he spoke to me again in the way he had done the previous day, it would end badly; and it would be likely I would want to settle our differences with a fist-fight. He shook me by the hand, saying: "O.K., we'll never talk about this again". We became good friends again, but I must admit that I was still a bit angry over the next few days. Whereas I always lost against Andres Gomez, I then went on to crush him. He was greatly amused as he had witnessed my set-to with Vilas. In the middle of the second set, after I had hit an unreturnable smash, he yelled out: "Hey, Mansour, I haven't done anything to you! There's no need to get upset." Those words took the sting out of the situation, but I finished the match on song, and I got through to the final. In that final I was beaten narrowly by Jimmy Connors.

**At an evening organised by Peter Worth (who is on the left): with
Amalia Nastase, Ilie's wife, and Mrs Worth.**

Chapter Twenty-Six

ROLLS-ROYCE

In 1995 I was voted Player of the Year on the Seniors' Tour, ahead of Borg, McEnroe and the others. It was a crowning glory for me. Beyond that kind of award, beyond even the victories, it's the trust put in me by the tournament organisers that makes me proud of my career. Peter Worth and his colleague Patrick Carr, for example, have been inviting me since 1992 to the tournaments they organise at Hurlingham, in London, Dublin, Manchester, Singapore and Hong Kong. These are elite events on the Seniors' Tour where only the best players are invited. We are greeted like heads of state. In Manchester, for example, the tournament has been sponsored by Rolls-Royce, and every player had a chauffeur-driven Phantom at his disposal during the tournament.

I have reflected back, more than once, to my childhood, as I have settled comfortably into the deep leather upholstery of one of these cars, transport of choice for so many of the world's grandest people. It's incredible how life can take you on strange turns, leading to places you could never imagine you would go, even in your wildest dreams. The lad from Amjadieh, forbidden to step foot on the tennis courts, came through to play matches against Borg and McEnroe; and was now cruising along in a Rolls-Royce ....

In Europe it doesn't matter much if you're treated like a prince, things never really get out of proportion. In India, on the other hand, it's on a whole different scale. I remember being in a tournament on the sub-continent organised by Vijay Amritraj, the former player from India. We took a plane from London and, upon landing at Mumbai, our 747 stopped dead in the middle of the runway, as we were told that we were the only ones allowed to disembark. Limousines were waiting for us on the tarmac to take us to the hotel, without our ever even passing through customs.

There were about two hundred journalists at the press conference.

Three days later we took off for Bangalore, and there, too, cars came to pick us up directly from the tarmac before the plane had reached the terminal. Instead of the limousines of Mumbai we had classic cars of the nineteen-twenties and thirties belonging to the local sultan. They were cars you don't see nowadays except in films, Bugattis, Rolls-Royces, gleaming brightly, every one. Each player had a car and a driver, and we went along in a kind of motorcade, with a dozen police motorcyclists at the front. At the side of the road, school kids waved little flags and sang their welcoming songs to us.

This excess of luxury and indulgence sometimes became annoying, even ridiculous. In Zagreb, Croatia, us players had been invited to dinner by the president of the republic, Franjo Tudjman. We arrived in the centre of town, surrounded by military vehicles and driven through a pedestrian precinct protected by snipers. The restaurant had been closed to everyone except us. We were very impressed, and the beginning of the meal was a bit stiff and formal. McEnroe and Borg were on either side of the president, but he replied to any of their questions with a simple yes or no. For once, McEnroe plumbed his depths of politeness to try to establish some rapport. Tudjman, however, looked blank and didn't seem to understand what was being said to him. That lasted about an hour, until finally Borg stood up in the middle of the meal and said: "O.K., I've had enough of this charade, I'm off!" And he left! He left under the bemused gaze of the officials at the neighbouring tables, who were keeping a wary eye on their president.

The end of the meal was pathetic. McEnroe turned his back on Tudjman to talk to Guy Forget and me. We were all ignoring the chap who was supposed to embody the authority of his nation. We couldn't care less about him, but he didn't seem to realise it. He remained there, silent, hardly moving while he ate. He was a living mummy, and to this day I don't know why he invited us. It was a pity, because Croatia has a strong tennis culture, with excellent players and an enthusiastic public. But the first among Croats, may his soul rest in peace, didn't appear to have the same energy as most of his compatriots.

At the official dinner in Croatia. The atmosphere is gloomy. I am with Henri and the others, trying to liven up the occasion.

I have savoured these rare moments when my profession has allowed me to live in extraordinary circumstances. It's true I have enjoyed luxury, but my best memories are not necessarily to be found there. It's the fits of laughter I've enjoyed with Noah and Leconte which have given me the most warmth. One such occasion was a tournament in Tokyo when Borg, Andres Gomez, Yannick, Henri and I were out in discos until dawn practically every night. After three or four nights like that we weren't on top form on court. This was especially true for Henri Leconte who missed the ball on the first point of a doubles match he was playing with Borg against Gomez and me: it was a pathetic, beginner's miss. Noah, who had supposedly come to support us from the stands, began laughing so violently that the whole crowd laughed too. It's not often you can unleash a collective laughing fit from a Japanese crowd. But we did. Even if our technical skills didn't reach the heights that day, the spectators left well contented. That's the sort of anecdote I will cherish when I come to end my career. I will remember the fiestas we had in New York, London, Los Angeles and Paris, most often with Yannick.

We met the French singer Michel Polnareff in a restaurant in Los Angeles. We talked for ages before he invited us to finish off the evening with him. He sat down at the piano, and we sang till dawn …. Just as I was beginning to nod off, Michel remembered that I had told him earlier in the evening that I loved his song "Marilou", and he dedicated it to me before singing it, just for me. Those are the sublime moments. I have experienced quite a few, and everything I have endured has been worth it, just for those moments.

Chapter Twenty-Seven

RETURN TO IRAN

I was playing in Grasse on Thursday 4th August 1983, almost three years to the day since my departure from Iran. My sleep had been disturbed for several weeks by a recurring nightmare in which I saw my father dying. I would wake up in tears. My mother and my brother had been saying for several days, in answer to my request for news, that everything was fine. But strangely, every time I called, he had gone out to the mosque, to visit one of his other sons or to visit friends. On that 4th August I was talking to my brother Shirzad and I raised the tone of my voice: "You're lying to me: something is happening to Papa, and I want to know what it is." There was a long, anguished silence, and he murmured: "Papa's not well. If you want to see him one last time, you'd better hurry up and come."

I went straight back to Paris and took the first flight to Tehran.

At Tehran airport there were more than thirty people waiting for me. The atmosphere was strange. I hadn't gone home for three years. Everyone was very happy to see me, but we all knew I had come back to see my dying father.

He was confined to bed, in his room, unconscious and on a drip. When I had left three years earlier he had weighed about eighty kilos and been about one metre seventy-seven. Now, hunched up on his mattress, he couldn't have weighed more than thirty-five or forty kilos. It was Ramadan and his obstinacy was what killed him.

That year Ramadan came in the month of July, and the fasting was really difficult to sustain, as one couldn't eat until sunset. My father had been suffering for a year from prostate cancer, and his condition worsened in the spring. His doctor, as well as the cleric at his mosque, had urged him not to fast, so as not to make his condition worse. There are dispensations from fasting in the Islamic texts for people who are ill. My father wouldn't have stepped out of line as far as his religion was concerned if he had spared himself this ordeal: but he had apparently rejected all this advice, saying: "I have observed Ramadan since I was a small child, and I have never given up my duty as a Muslim; and I am not going to start looking for excuses to avoid fasting now that I am eighty-four and nearing the end of my time on this earth." He was determined.

The doctor was right. My father observed Ramadan and never recovered. Seeing him so weakened, my eyes filled with tears. My mother whispered in his ear: "Rahim, Mansour is here." He opened his eyes, but with pain. He was crying. I went close to him and heard his voice, as gentle as a light breeze: "Mansour, it's been a long time."

Those were his last words. Three days later, as I was visiting friends, the telephone rang. I don't know who told me, but I have the words etched in my memory: "It's over. He's died."

There is only one cemetery in Tehran, in the south of the city. That's where my father's remains lie. He was buried, as a good Muslim should be, the day after his death, wrapped in a white shroud. Seven or eight hundred people came to pay their last respects to him. The women were howling, my mother was completely distraught. As for me, I was lost in my memories.

I could see him again when, at the age of seventy, he had finally been able to retire. He had become rather embittered at not working any longer. He often lost his temper, and if one contradicted him, he would usually sink himself further into his wrong-headedness. I was thinking there, in this vast cemetery, of the day he tore up the vines which grew in the garden and which had yielded such delicious grapes. I had come to visit him and, when I arrived, I saw him tearing into a vine. I asked him why he was doing it, and he wouldn't reply. When my mother joined in, trying to persuade him to give up his miserable task, he lost his temper and tore at the remaining stems. Later, he watered the weeds. Today I can smile looking back on this episode but, at the time, I was at my wits' end.

My mother's tears drew me out of my recollections. I came up to her and held her in my arms. She began talking to me about him and about our life when I was a child.

She was always worried about me. Every time I went to swim in the pool she was afraid I would drown. I had to wait for her to turn her back before I went to find my swimming trunks. Even so, she knew I swam like a fish.

She reminded me of the day I played a trick for some reason I no longer remember. She wanted to give me a spanking, so I ran off into the park, but she was hot on my heels. She tore her knee as she ran and collapsed. I had turned round to ask her to give me the beating due to me but above all not to stay lying on the ground. I was in a blind panic that she would throw me out because of my fooling around. I was a fairly well-behaved and obedient kid but, like all children, enraged my parents quite often. That all ended with a clout from my father. I said yes to everything he said, not daring even to look him in the eyes. With her it was different. One day she was so exasperated listening to me making a noise in our little hovel where living at such close quarters drove the grown-ups crazy that she said to me: "I've had enough of you lot, I'm leaving." And off she went, into the snow. She was playing games with me but, at the time, I wasn't sure of anything. I left the house after her, in my shorts and barefoot, in the snow. I fastened myself to her overcoat, crying, begging her to come back. She went on for at least five hundred yards, as far as the butcher's shop, at the entrance to Amjadieh. There she gave me a lecture and made me promise to behave better in future. I promised everything she demanded. I was blue with cold, and my teeth were chattering. She took pity on me, and after she had done her shopping, we went home together.

For the death of my father I stayed five weeks in Tehran, hardly practising at all. I played only once, in a little doubles tournament, because my friend Kambiz asked me to. I was so far away from tennis. When I got back to France, I thought I must have put on five or six kilos. I was exhausted. In fact, I had lost twelve! They were shed through sadness.

It took two years before I could go back to Tehran. The city had changed so much that I didn't recognise anything any more. I felt lost there.

Before the revolution there had been not quite two million inhabitants; the air had been clean then, and in summer as in winter you could see the mountains behind the city. The colours were magnificent, and you often saw horse-drawn carts in the streets.

Now there are twenty million people there, the air is polluted, and you can't make out the line of the mountain tops. There are highways and motorways everywhere. The millions of cars using them are stinking hulks spewing out a stifling haze. There are hardly any more green spaces. The clothes shops display all the conceivable fashions, but only in grey and black. Colour seems to have been banned. Thousands of drug addicts roam the streets. Heroin and opium imported for next to nothing from Afghanistan are taking a terrible toll. You walk past zombies, their skin blackened like people infected with the plague, so skinny they look close to death. Indeed they do die, on the pavements. One's only recreation seems to be taking tea with friends, men on one side, women on the other.

Despite this melancholy backdrop I have gone back to Iran practically every year since 1992. It's where I come from.

With my sons I have even come across the giant who tried to kill me that day when I was brazen enough to set foot on the clay courts of Amjadieh. Sam wanted to punch him in the face. I counselled forgiveness.

Chapter Twenty-Eight

THE FUTURE

What will become of me? I haven't asked myself the question for a long time, not since the time when I was wandering around the streets of Paris at night. The future doesn't hold any terror for me any more. I do have a few health worries, such as creaking joints in the mornings, like all high performance athletes, but I feel deep inside me a sense of serenity, of duty fulfilled and of an active life which both reassures and calms me. Soon, for sure, I will have to sit and watch while the younger ones take over the playing. What will I do then? Perhaps I'll go more often to Tehran? If the political situation improves, I will try to organise tennis matches there, exhibition matches, a veterans' tournament with my friends from the circuit, or perhaps an ATP competition. I'm not sure: we'll see …. I have named my new dog, a beautiful boxer, Darya, which means the sea in Persian.

One thing is certain. I will go on organising the Trophy of the Roland-Garros Legends, which takes place during the French Open, as I have been doing since 1997. That idea had been turning around in my mind since 1992. I didn't see why the Parisian crowd shouldn't have the pleasure of seeing the tournament champions of yesteryear meeting in doubles and singles matches between the contests played by the younger ones. The tournament director at the time, Patrice Clerc, was doubtful about the prospects for success of that kind of venture, as indeed a similar attempt had failed in 1983. Finally, the president of the French Tennis Federation, Christian Bîmes, insisted on my trying to revive the idea. Patrice Clerc eventually agreed, in 1997: "Mansour, you've got me to the stage where I'm fed up with this idea, so go ahead and give it a try. If it doesn't work, you'll drop it, O.K.?" We shook hands on it, and I sent out the invitations. I invited my best friends: Yannick Noah, Ilie Nastase, Henri Leconte, Andrès Gomez, John McEnroe, Gene Meyer, Guy Forget; plus some other glorious veterans such as Tony Roche, John Newcombe, Ken Rosewall and Manolo Santana.

The whole Bahrami family, with our former bitch Nasty, christened in honour of the great Ilie Nastase.

When Patrice Clerc saw the outcome, the size of the crowd in the stands and the pleasure they seemed to derive from seeing us play, he said: "It's unbelievable! You were right, Mansour, and we'll do the same again next year." It's fair to point out too, that there have been more people there sometimes, to see us play, than are watching on another court, certain matches in the French Open itself.

In 1997, Guy Forget and I reached the doubles final, to play John McEnroe and Henri Leconte on the Roland-Garros number one court in front of a jubilant crowd overflowing from the stands. As Guy and I reached the heights of two match points, at 6 – 4, 5 – 4 (and 40 – 15), Christain Bîmes started to get the trophy ready, as it seemed obvious he would be presenting it to us a couple of minutes later. McEnroe saw that and was wound up: he psyched up Leconte, and they won the next four points with some incredible shots. In the mayhem they carried off the second set. Mac then shouted across to Bîmes: "Hey, Christian, get lost and come back in an hour. They haven't skinned us yet."

In the kind of atmosphere you get at the Davis Cup, we reached a tie-break in the concluding set. Guy and I had two or three match points, which we weren't able to convert into a win. Our luck turned. I hit the last volley out. Straightaway a horrible thought crossed my mind: "I'll never win in a final at Roland-Garros."

I was wrong. On a gleaming summer's day, in May 2002, I lifted the Legends trophy above my head on the Suzanne Lenglen court.

Every time I think about it I hear the cheers of encouragement from my son Antoine and his childhood friend Charles who regards me as his uncle, and Hugo, my godson. In a moment of silence when we were changing ends, they had made the whole crowd laugh by shouting, in quick succession: "Go on, dad!" "Go on, uncle!" and "Go on, godfather!"

When I was ten, in the paradise that was Amjadieh, I imagined myself as a champion at Roland-Garros, lifting my trophy up high in front of an applauding public. Of course, I was thinking of the trophy awarded for the winner of the French Open; but when I think about it a bit more deeply, there have been crazy twists and turns in my life which somehow led me to the moment when I actually fulfilled my childhood dreams at the grand old age of forty-six.

At last! At the age of forty-seven, I win a title at Roland-Garros… the Legends Tournament, with my partner Gene Meyer.

For many years now, as the British tennis-playing public have come to expect, each December I have been invited to play at the Royal Albert Hall in London in the Blackrock Masters Veterans Tournament. I love performing there, it has a very special atmosphere. A unique place, in fact, to play tennis, with its ornate gold décor and plush red velvet seats; men in tuxedoes and women in long dresses dine in their boxes and you can hear the clink of champagne glasses on court. The crowd claps and cheers and really gets into the spirit of the occasion. To be part of such a line-up comprising past Wimbledon champions and other great players is a privilege and the artistic history of the Royal Albert Hall itself is enough to inspire me.

I also never miss the opportunity to play in the Veterans events at Wimbledon where, of course, new tennis history is made every year.

Now in my fifties, my passion for tennis is undiminished and I continue to play as much as ever and I hope still entertain the crowds….

At the final of the Seniors' Tour Masters doubles final at the Albert Hall in London in December 2004. With Patrick Carr, the organiser, and Boris Becker, my partner in this tournament.

«At the finals of the 2008 Seniors' Tour at the Royal Albert Hall. From left to right, Mark Woodforde, Peter McNamara, me, and Peter Fleming.»

Acknowledgements

Thanks to Olivier Devismes who encouraged me to write this book

To Yann and Ilie for their kind words at the beginning of the book

To Dr Montalvan who has looked after my health for many years.

A big thank you to Jean Issartel

Thanks too to my sponsors Head and Lacoste who have supported me for so many years

To Gianni Ciaccia, Peter Haucke, Tim Edwards and Bertrand Rindoff-Petroff, all great photographers

An English thank you to Nigel Forrest who translated my book from French into English and to Ros Edwards who organised its publication

And a big thank you to all the players on the world circuit who have helped me become what I am

Photo Credits

Thanks to the following copyright owners for permission to reproduce their photographs in this book:

Angeli Agency, Tim Edwards, Peter Haucke, Gianni Ciaccia, Art Seitz and the Mansour Bahrami Collection.

"Standing outside the Royal Albert Hall in December 2005,
what an arena!"